WILD MARINE ANIMALS!

MANATEES

Melissa and Brandon Cole

BLACKBIRCH PRESS, INC.
WOODBRIDGE, CONNECTICUT

Published by Blackbirch Press, Inc.
260 Amity Road
Woodbridge, CT 06525

Email: staff@blackbirch.com
Web site: www.blackbirch.com

©2001 by Blackbirch Press, Inc.
First Edition

Printed in China

Photo Credits: All images ©Brandon D. Cole, except pages 8 and 9: ©Doug Perrine/Innerspace Visions.

10 9 8 7 6 5 4 3 2 1

Library of Congress Cataloging-in-Publication Data
Cole, Melissa S.
Manatees / by Melissa S. Cole.
     p. cm. — (Wild marine animals!)
ISBN 1-56711-445-8 (hardcover)
1. Manatees—Juvenile literature. [1. Manatees.]   I. Title.
QL737.S63 C65   2001
599.55—dc21

00-013064

Contents

Introduction

Manatees are large plant-eating marine mammals. They spend their whole lives in water. Long before people knew what manatees were, sailors mistook them for beautiful mermaids. That seems hard to believe! Sometimes captains on sailing ships would see the heads of manatees bobbing on the surface of the ocean and think that they were people who had fallen overboard.

Today, we are lucky enough to know a good deal about these animals, such as where they are found and how they live. Many people even visit special manatee parks to enjoy watching these magical creatures in their natural habitats.

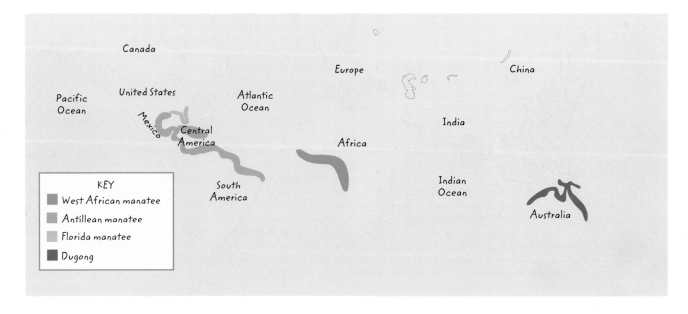

Canada

Europe   China

Pacific   United States   Atlantic
Ocean   Ocean
                Mexico   India

                Central
                America   Africa

                                                         Indian
                South   Ocean
KEY   America
West African manatee   Australia
Antillean manatee
Florida manatee
Dugong

Manatees, and dugongs, relatives of manatees, belong to a group called "Sirenians." These animals once lived all over the world. For centuries, they were hunted for food, oil, and leather. Only four species survive today.

Does this manatee look like a beautiful mermaid? Sailors long ago thought so.

Members of the Family

West Indian Manatees

West Indian Manatees are studied more than any other Sirenian. There are two types, or "sub-species," of West Indian Manatees. The first are Antillean Manatees, which are found throughout the Caribbean Islands and as far south as Brazil. The second are the Florida Manatees, which are found around Florida's coastal waters. Florida Manatees can range as far south as Texas and as far north as Rhode Island. Both Florida and Antillean manatees can grow up to 13 feet (4 meters) long and can weigh up to 3,500 pounds (1,587 kilograms).

Some manatees like to wander more than others do. In 1994, an adult male named Chessie became famous when he swam more than 500 miles (310 km)—all the way from Florida to Maryland's Chesapeake Bay! That journey broke all

Some kinds of manatees live in the waters around islands in the Caribbean Sea.

Florida manatees live in warm waters near the coast of Florida.

known manatee swimming records. Scientists flew Chessie home in an Air Force plane and put a radio-tracking collar on him to see where he would go. The next summer, he swam past the Chesapeake Bay all the way to Rhode Island. He returned that winter—without the help of a plane—to the warm springs of Crystal River, Florida.

Dugongs live in seagrass meadows in the Pacific and Indian Oceans.

Amazonian Manatees

These animals live in hidden fresh water rivers in the Amazon Basin of South America. They are extremely rare. They only grow to 9 feet (3 meters) in length and are the smallest of all manatees.

West African Manatees

West African Manatees live in the quiet coastal lagoons, lakes, and rivers of more than 20 different African countries. They are difficult to find—they live in areas that are hard to reach for humans. Their bodies are most like those of the West Indian Manatees.

Dugongs have tails shaped like the tails of dolphins.

Dugongs

Dugongs live in the tropics of the Indian and Pacific oceans. Most of them are found in the seagrass meadows off Northern Australia and Papua New Guinea. Dugongs are quite different than manatees. They only grow to about 6 feet (2 meters) long, which is half the size of an average manatee. Dugongs have smooth skin and "fluked" tails like dolphins, instead of paddle-like tails. Male dugongs even grow short tusks, unlike manatees. These tusks grow out between their lips and are used to fight for females during the mating season.

Dugongs are most similar to the Steller's Sea Cow, which went extinct about 200 years ago. Humans killed all of them for meat.

The Body of a Manatee

Manatees look a bit like chubby seals. They have large, tubular bodies and short flippers instead of arms. On the ends of their flippers they have "fingernails," like the nails on an elephant's foot. Scientists think that elephants and manatees might have shared a common ancestor millions of years ago.

Manatees' broad paddle-shaped tails push them through the water. **Inset:** Manatees have "fingernails" on the ends of their flippers.

Amazonian Manatees are the only manatees to have "lost" their fingernails.

Although manatees usually move quite slowly, their broad paddle-shaped tails help them swim fast when they need to. They can grow up to 13 feet (4 meters) long and weigh as much as 3,500 pounds (1,587 kilograms). Manatees have thick, leathery, grayish-brown skin with just a few hairs poking out. Sometimes it's difficult for them to see in the muddy, murky waters where they live. The hairs on their skin help them feel what's around.

Manatees have funny round heads with squinty eyes and whiskery lips. Some people have described them as "smiling potatoes with flippers."

A manatee's nose and chin are covered with whiskers that help it feel what is nearby.

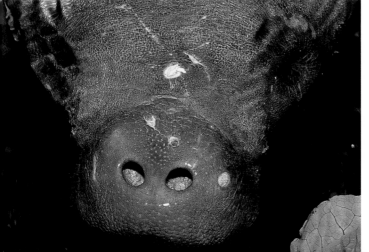

Special Features

Manatees have some interesting features that enable them to spend their entire lives in water.

Manatees are experts at controlling the amount of air in their lungs. When their lungs are full, they can float easily to the surface. When their lungs are not full, they sink. Manatees have very heavy bones that help them sink when they want to. Manatee nostrils are like submarine valves. They open when the animal needs to breathe, and clamp shut when the animal goes under-water. In fact, manatees can only breathe through their noses. This means they can eat below the water's surface without drowning. They don't ever "swallow water down the

Top: Manatees can eat without swallowing water. **Bottom:** A manatee's nostrils open above water and then shut when it goes underwater.

wrong tube" like humans do because their tubes aren't joined together.

There is one more special feature that manatee bodies have. When manatees sleep, half of their brain actually stays awake to make sure that they keep coming up for air!

In photographs, a manatee's eyes often

The membrane over this manatee's eyes makes it look sleepy.

appear dull and lifeless. That is because of a membrane that protects their eyes underwater. It's a feature they also share with sharks.

A thin layer of fat just beneath their skin helps manatees stay warm in water. Even though manatees might look fat, they don't have as much blubber as other marine mammals. If a manatee gets too cold, it can easily become sick. In the cool winter months, they must migrate from the sea to warmer freshwater springs in rivers, where they rest and feed. In the summertime, manatees are usually found traveling in saltwater along a coastline.

Food

Manatees are the only plant-eating marine mammals alive today. They graze on seagrass and other water plants, such as hydrilla and water hyacinth. Most manatees graze for more than eight hours a day. This explains why they have been nicknamed "eating machines" or "sea cows!" Their intestines, which can be as long as 130 feet (40 meters), help them digest the 150 pounds (68 kilograms) of water plants they gobble every day.

A manatee's mouth is made for munching.

Manatee mouths are made to munch. Their upper lips are split down the middle and move independently of each other. These flexible lips can grab and pull plants into their mouths. Manatees also have special bony plates in the front of their mouths and wide, flat molars in the back to help grind up stringy plants before swallowing.

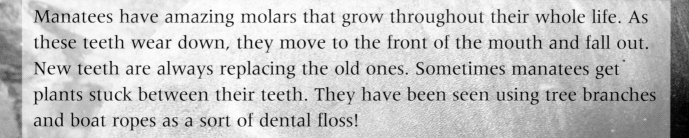

Manatees have amazing molars that grow throughout their whole life. As these teeth wear down, they move to the front of the mouth and fall out. New teeth are always replacing the old ones. Sometimes manatees get plants stuck between their teeth. They have been seen using tree branches and boat ropes as a sort of dental floss!

Manatees are "eating machines"— they eat more than eight hours a day.

Social Life

Unlike many animals, manatees don't fight for mates or places to live. While they seem to enjoy each other's company, they don't need to travel in large herds for protection because they don't have any natural enemies. During most of the year, manatees travel alone or in small groups of two and three. They gently play together, tumbling and rolling, grabbing each other's flippers and using their rubbery lips to nuzzle one another in what looks like a big manatee "kiss."

Left: Manatees like to play with each other.
Opposite: Manatees often sleep together in warm waters.

Manatees often gather into groups to enjoy Florida's warm, freshwater springs. Some animals even crowd near power plants, where warm water flows out into the ocean. It is not uncommon to see a group of manatees sleeping together underwater. They communicate with each other with squeaks, chirps, and whistles. Groups of manatees use different types of noises to welcome an arriving manatee, to say good-bye, or to signal danger. Scientists think that manatees can make, and hear, very soft sounds no louder than a whisper.

The Mating Game

Manatees can live more than 60 years. Females usually start having babies when they are around five years old. Females give birth every two to five years, and sometimes have twins. When a female is ready to mate, males come from far away and follow her around. Sometimes, more than 30 males will tag alongside a female, and will stay for up to a month. This usually happens in the spring. A female will often choose to mate with more than one male. Her pregnancy lasts about 13 months. This means the baby is born the next spring when the water is starting to warm. Once a baby (called a calf) is born, the mother takes care of it by herself.

Left: Male manatees come from far away to find a mate.

Opposite: Males and females will embrace in a courtship hug.

Raising Young

Calves are usually born tail first in quiet backwater canals and river channels. They are about four feet (1.2 meters) long and weigh from 60 to 70 pounds (27.2 to 31.7 kilograms). The first thing a newborn does is swim to the surface for a breath of air. Mother manatees often support their calves at the surface until they get used to breathing on their own. Soon after birth, a calf will begin to nurse underwater from one of its mother's two nipples. These nipples are found under the mother's flipper. When babies nurse, it looks like they're attached to their mother's armpit! Calves aren't born with much blubber to keep them warm or help them float. To help them gain weight quickly, babies need to drink plenty of rich, fatty, milk.

Top: Manatee calves stay with their mothers for about two years.
Bottom: A baby manatee nurses underwater.

Calves often return to visit their mothers when they become adults.

Even though they learn to start eating plants within weeks of their birth, calves will nurse and stay with their mothers for nearly two years. Mother manatees teach their calves which plants to eat, where to find warm waters for the winter, and how to escape danger.

Female manatees appear to be very kind. They often "adopt" orphaned calves that have lost their mothers. In these cases a "step-mom" may even care for her adopted calf as well as her own newborn. The bond between mothers and their young is very strong. Calves often return to be with their mothers even when they have grown up.

Manatees and Humans

Manatees and their habitats are endangered. This means they are in danger of disappearing. In parts of the Caribbean, West Indian Manatees are still hunted for their meat, skin, bones, and blubber. In Florida, many people drive boats. Sometimes, when boats are going too fast, manatees can't hear them in time to get out of the way. During some years, over 100 manatees have died from being hit by boats.

Manatees are naturally friendly. They will often follow swimmers. They even like to have their bellies and armpits rubbed softly!

These marks were made by a boat propeller.

Manatees are naturally friendly.

Many people around the world are trying hard to save manatees and their habitats from extinction. The "Save the Manatee" club helps to set aside "manatee-only" areas where manatees can rest away from people and boats. They are trying to pass laws that make boat drivers go slower in special manatee areas. Motorboats would also have devices that would warn manatees that a boat was coming.

In an effort to help save manatees, scientists are attaching radio collars, which fit around a manatee's tail, when captured or previously sick animals are released. This helps researchers study travel patterns and keep track of how many manatees remain in the wild. Hopefully, with enough people helping, manatee populations will increase and humans will be able to enjoy these special creatures for many years to come.

West Indian Manatee Facts

Scientific Name: Trichechus manatus

Body Length: Up to 13 feet (4 meters) long

Weight: Up to 3,500 pounds (1,587 kilograms)

Color: Brownish gray

Reaches sexual maturity: 5 years

Gestation: 13 months

Calves Born: Usually 1 calf born every 2 to 3 years

Favorite Food: Water plants, such as Water Hyacinth and Hydrilla

Range: Throughout the Caribbean and along the Florida Coast

GLOSSARY

blubber The fat under the skin of a manatee, whale, or seal.

extinct When a plant or animal has died out.

habitat The place and natural condition in which a plant or animal lives.

migrate To travel when seasons change.

molar A broad, flat tooth at the back of the mouth used for grinding food.

species A group of similar animals.

FOR MORE INFORMATION

Books

Feeney, Kathy. *Manatees* (Our Wild World). Minnetonka, MN: Creative Publishing International, 2001.

Perry, Phyllis Jean. *Freshwater Giants: Hippopotamus, River Dolphins, and Manatees.* Danbury, CT: Franklin Watts, Inc., 1999.

Ripple, Jeff. *Manatees and Dugongs of the World.* Stillwater, MN: Voyageur Press, 1999.

Walker, Sally M. *Manatees.* Minneapolis, MN: Lerner Publishing Group, 1999.

Web Site

Manatees

Learn more about a manatee's habitat, physical characteristics, and behavior—
www.seaworld.org/manatee/manatees.html

INDEX

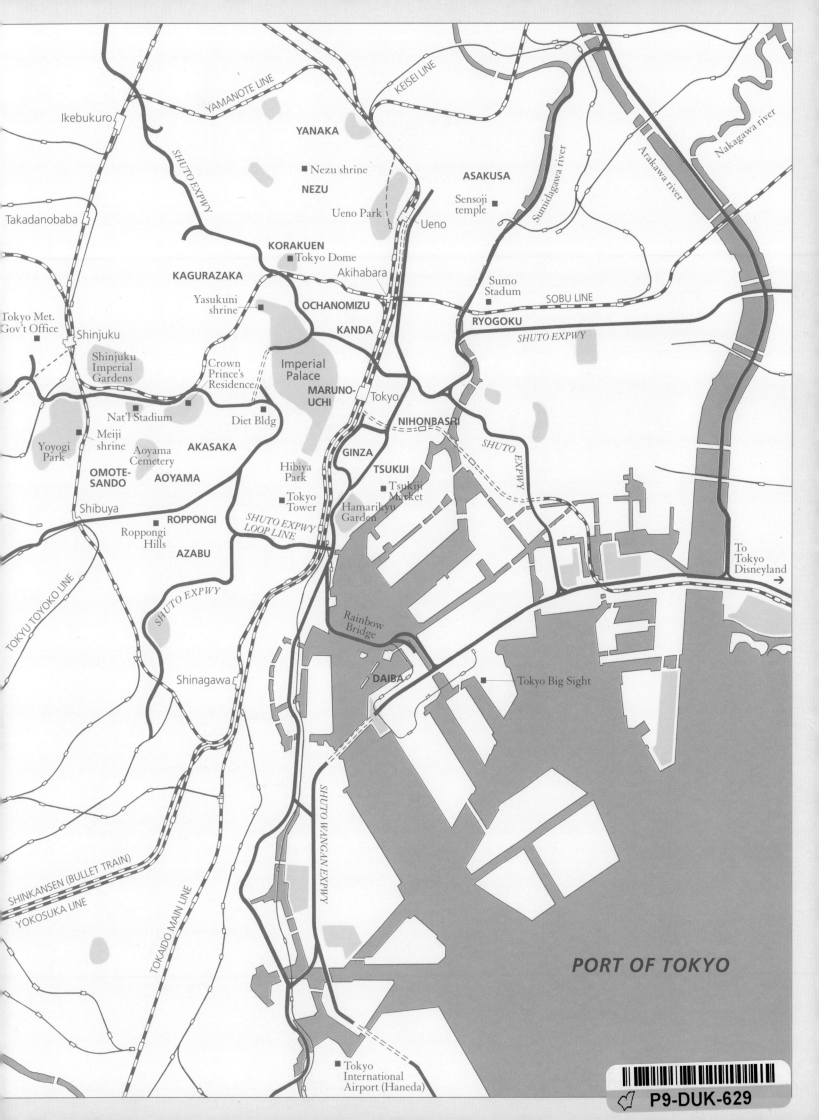

Ikebukuro

Takadanobaba

YAMANOTE LINE

KEISEI LINE

Nakagawa river

YANAKA

■ Nezu shrine

ASAKUSA

NEZU

Arakawa river

Sumidagawa river

Ueno Park

■ Sensoji temple

Ueno

KORAKUEN

■ Tokyo Dome

Akihabara

KAGURAZAKA

OCHANOMIZU

Sumo Stadium

SOBU LINE

Yasukuni shrine ■

KANDA

RYOGOKU

Tokyo Met. Gov't Office ■

Shinjuku

SHUTO EXPWY

Shinjuku Imperial Gardens

Crown Prince's Residence

Imperial Palace

MARUNO-UCHI

Tokyo

SHUTO EXPWY

NIHONBASHI

Nat'l Stadium ■

Diet Bldg ■

GINZA

Meiji shrine ■

Yoyogi Park

AKASAKA

TSUKIJI

Aoyama Cemetery

Hibiya Park

■ Tsukiji Market

OMOTE-SANDO

AOYAMA

■ Tokyo Tower

Shibuya

Hamarikyu Garden

ROPPONGI

Roppongi Hills

SHUTO EXPWY LOOP LINE

AZABU

To Tokyo Disneyland →

TOKYU TOYOKO LINE

SHUTO EXPWY

Rainbow Bridge

Shinagawa

DAIBA

■ Tokyo Big Sight

SHUTO WANGAN EXPWY

SHINKANSEN (BULLET TRAIN)

YOKOSUKA LINE

TOKAIDO MAIN LINE

PORT OF TOKYO

■ Tokyo International Airport (Haneda)

SEEING
TOKYO

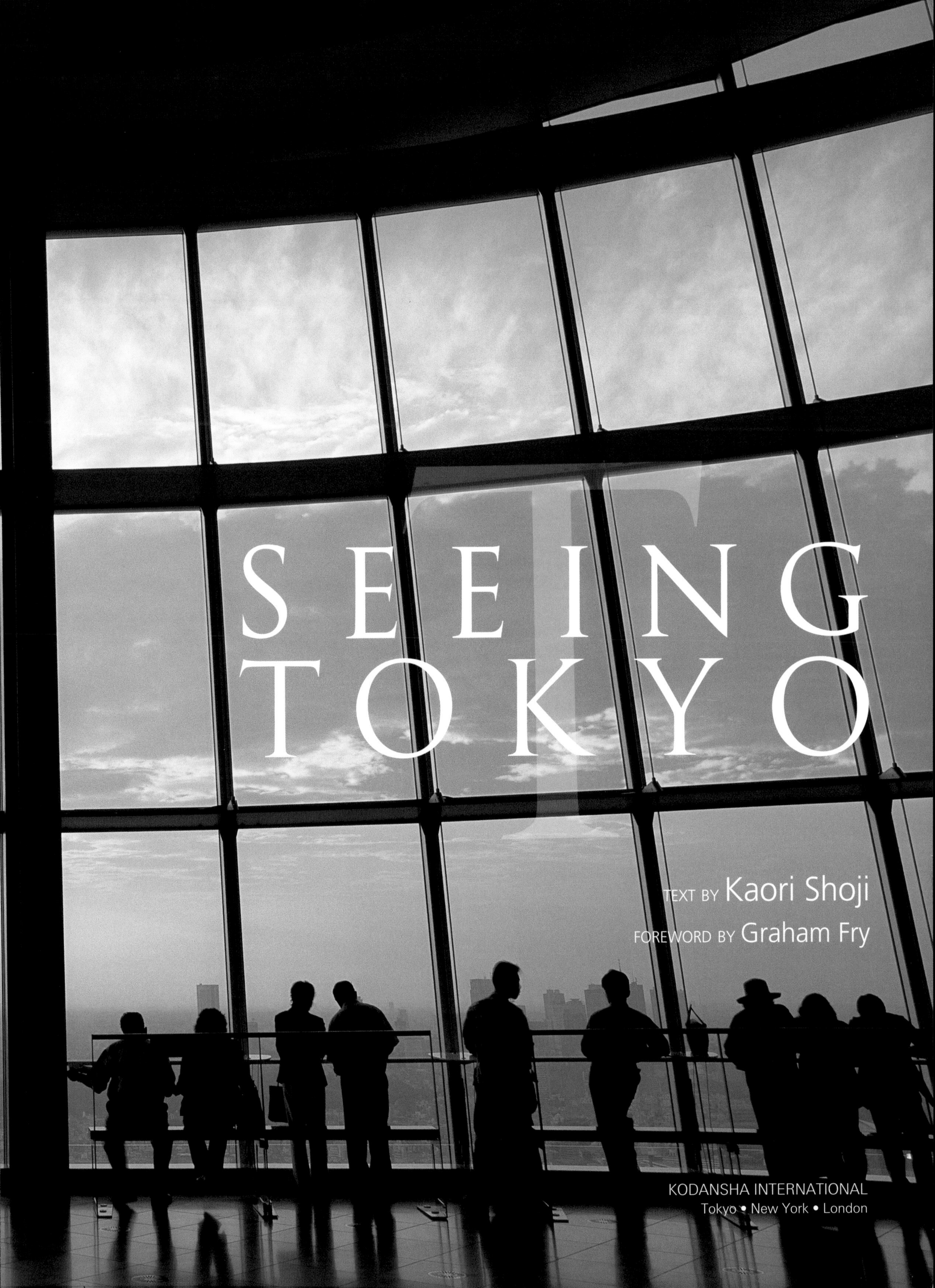

SEEING TOKYO

TEXT BY Kaori Shoji

FOREWORD BY Graham Fry

KODANSHA INTERNATIONAL
Tokyo • New York • London

Distributed in the United States by Kodansha America, Inc., and in the United Kingdom and continental Europe by Kodansha Europe Ltd.

Published by Kodansha International Ltd., 17–14 Otowa 1-chome, Bunkyo-ku, Tokyo 112–8652, and Kodansha America, Inc.

First edition, 2005
15 14 13 12 11 10 09 08   10 9 8 7 6 5 4

www.kodansha-intl.com

PAGES 2–3: Around Shinbashi, dusk is the most beautiful time.
PAGES 4–5: Viewing the Tokyo skyline from Roppongi.
PAGES 6–7: Old and new—it is all Tokyo. Everything has been designed with utter precision.

ABOVE: The hub for domestic flights—Haneda Airport. RIGHT, FROM TOP: Tokyo streets provide some of the world's most amazing views—the Fuji Television Headquarters in Odaiba, a daytime street crossing, the River City 21 Condominiums.

CONTENTS

FOREWORD

Graham Fry

Tokyo is one of the world's greatest cities. It was bigger than London as far back as the eighteenth century and is now the heart of the world's second largest economy. For energy and originality it can have few competitors. Perhaps this book will encourage more people to come and have a look.

I enjoy guiding newcomers around Tokyo, but there is a perennial difficulty—where to begin? There is no simple answer for the visitor who has a free day in the city and wants advice on what to see.

Part of the problem is that Tokyo has no iconic symbols like the Eiffel Tower in Paris or the White House in Washington. Earthquakes, fires, and war have wreaked great destruction. They have spared the Meiji Shrine and the temple at Asakusa, which are well worth a visit. So are the Cyclopean walls of the Imperial Palace, crowned with pine trees and ancient towers and surrounded by moats. These historic sites are where newcomers to Tokyo often go first; but none of them really defines the city.

Sometimes it is a modern icon which comes to symbolize a city. The Petronas Twin Towers in Kuala Lumpur, where I lived for three years, are one example. From time to time Tokyo also boasts a spectacular new building, which becomes the place for everyone to visit and admire. Since I first came to Tokyo in 1974 most buildings seem to have been torn down and rebuilt, some of them twice. Almost always the quality of the new is higher than that of the old. The skyline of central Tokyo ("What skyline?" some people used to ask) can now hold its own with that of other great cities. The visitor now gets a first glimpse of it when being driven into central Tokyo over the new reclaimed area in the bay.

So another answer to my visitors is to seek out something new. The people of this city have always loved the newest fashion, the latest play, the most original cuisine. It now has superb concert halls and galleries where the world's greatest art can be seen and heard. It is the home of Japan's manga books and animé films. Its shops, regularly rebuilt and redesigned, have the latest fashions from the most famous brands. The Japanese still love good food of all kinds, preferably a variety of dishes, each exquisitely presented.

So there is plenty of choice for those who wish to enjoy the good things in life, and plenty of unusual experiences. Visitors can go to Akihabara to see the frenzy of the electronics shops and perhaps buy the very latest device. After the solemnity and tranquility of the Meiji shrine, the visitor need only take a few steps to be confronted by the extravagant young and their fashions in Harajuku on a Sunday afternoon.

Yet even this may not get to the heart of the matter. The more I have thought about it, the more I am led to conclude that the most remarkable thing about this city is probably its continuity. The buildings and the fashions change, but this is still recognizably Tokyo, and the customs and social structures endure.

I have always been fascinated, for example, at how, inside a grey modern concrete tower, sometimes even in the basement, Japanese restaurants can manage to create the illusion that you are in a traditional Japanese home with its tatami-mat floors and sliding screens. Sometimes you may even have to walk along a stone path "outside" before reaching the room where the food will be served. Similar is the placing of a Shinto shrine on top of a new building: the gods have moved vertically, but they are still there.

With its extensions north, east, and south, this city has over twenty-five million people. It could be a monster, but it works. The trains run on time. It is safe to walk the streets. It is still remarkably clean. People wait for the

pedestrian light to turn green before crossing the road. There is a mighty sense of order, and that derives from the mosaic of villages which Tokyo spread out to encompass. The secret of Tokyo is the sense of local community.

One of my predecessors quoted some Japanese architectural students in the 1960s as commenting that we in the West "were primarily concerned with the exteriors and were relatively uninterested in what went on inside. They would tend to view the matter, they said, from the inside out." Perhaps this gives a clue to the design of Tokyo. It also encapsulates the challenge for those of us who try from the outside to understand how it works.

Really to understand this city, therefore, means entering a local community, and that is not easy to do as a visitor. Perhaps the best approximation is to attend one of the events that make up the city's calendar—to visit the sumo wrestling for example during one of its three tournaments a year in Tokyo, to hunt out a boisterous local festival, or to join the crowds admiring the cherry blossoms (or another flower in bloom) at a favorite spot. All these things, and more, are pictured in the book. I hope you enjoy it.

Towering testimony to Tokyo's love for design,
the metropolitan government office buildings.

INTRODUCTION

Being a Tokyoite is not the same as being a New Yorker or a Parisian. The city possesses no distinguishing landmarks on par with the Statue of Liberty and the Arc de Triomphe, the people all seem like they are commuting from someplace else, and—most importantly—they do not seem all that interested in advertising their love and pride for Tokyo. For the many Japanese who come from other parts of the country, the city is simply a place to work and at the end of the day escape from; gratefully, they board a train that will take them away from the constant construction noises, narrow and haphazardly laid-out streets, the impossible traffic, and the high cost of living.

But for those born and bred here, Tokyo is home—for better or worse. I got my introduction to the true Tokyoite in a downtown neighborhood located on the banks of the Sumida River. My family lived in an antiquated apartment built just after the Great Kanto Earthquake of 1923, which meant the four of us were squeezed into two rooms. At night we tucked towels and small wash-bowls under our arms and went to the *sento* (public bath) across the street like everyone else. No one bothered to lock their doors, and children drifted in and out of other people's homes as they pleased; many week nights I had dinner at neighbors' homes and would sit watching TV with them until my mother came to retrieve me. Back in our apartment some neighbor or other would be smoking and talking with my father, and I would be sent to the corner grocer's for more cigarettes and some ice cream.

The apartment next to ours was occupied by an elderly couple whom we quite naturally referred to as Grandma and Grandpa. They were the first genuine Tokyoites I had observed up close: they had both been living in the neighborhood since birth and could trace their descendants back five generations. Grandma's great grandmother had served the shogun in court (her main job was to fold his kimonos), and subsequently Grandma had inherited a scroll bearing witness to her relative's service, stamped with the shogunate seal. I loved listening to the couple talk—their clipped Tokyo accent and particular lifestyle seemed to me the hallmarks of civilized behavior. Every morning Grandma would clean the entire apartment top to bottom, and polish the woodwork. She took special care in keeping the toilet spanking clean and professed that not even air raid sirens could stop her from this task ("If I was going to die in a fire-bombing, I could at least die knowing the house was clean," she would say). Breakfast was a classic Japanese meal of piping hot rice, miso soup, homemade pickles, and grilled fish. After that, there were more chores and then came the ritual of grocery shopping with a small, cute basket slung over her arm. Grandma never shopped in bulk since there was no need—all the local shops were close by and it was just not the done thing to walk around with a lot of stuff. She would start elaborate dinner preparations with her careful selection of the season's freshest fare at four in the afternoon, and by five-thirty a couple of Grandpa's friends would be over for beer and conversation. On weekends they sauntered over to the local movie house, the Kabuki Theater in Ginza, or Mitsukoshi Department Store in Nihonbashi. They secretly took pride in the fact that they almost never ventured more than a mile beyond their street, and in their whole lives had not traveled further west than the Hakone hot springs area southwest of Tokyo for a rare vacation. There was simply no need; the world began and ended in their neighborhood.

It was from this couple that I learned the traits and virtues of the true

Tokyoite. To sum up, real Tokyo locals always live in old, inner-city neighborhoods and know how to make the most of small spaces. They never ask for much, since material desire is one of the most cumbersome and tedious things in the world, and they have honed the art of understatement. Their worst enemies are exaggeration, excess, and loudness; they have a hearty contempt for public display. And though Tokyoites have a deep appreciation for the finer things in life, they do not go in for hoarding, whether it be money or luxury goods. Accordingly, Tokyoites are more prepared than most to waste good money on the most transitory of pleasures: coffee shops, flowers, movies, and magazines.

Tokyoites have been (rightly) accused of being too lightweight, blase, and flippant. They are also quick to give things up and wave the white flag—and have often proved themselves helpless against war and the urban development and redevelopment that has consistently torn up the city's fabric of daily living. This is because they would rather rely on indomitable optimism (another distinctly Tokyo trait) over putting up a fight, and feel fairly sure that the bumps—whether it be air raids, earthquakes, or out-of-town contractors with their noisy bulldozers—will be gone soon. Finally, Tokyoites can be short-tempered and sharp-tongued but their emotions rarely last beyond the moment.

All this has helped generations of Tokyoites survive in a city that is constantly changing, expanding, destroying, and then reinventing itself. In this city where houses, buildings, even entire neighborhoods do not last for very long, it is this sense of survival and the broadness of mind and heart to accept whatever urban fate awaits that describes the essence of the true born-and-bred Tokyoite.

Tokyo from above a maze of lights and high-tech.

The famed Kaminari-mon (Lightning Gate) at the entrance to the temple Senso-ji in Asakusa.

PART I

ASAKUSA, UENO, YANAKA, NEZU

Three things stir the heart of every true Tokyoite: *sento* (public baths), mazelike *roji* (alleys), and *matsuri* (festivals). Sadly, they have been on the endangered species list for some time, though there are still pockets in the megalopolis where all three can be found in miraculous coexistence. This happens most frequently in an area known as *shitamachi*, a term first coined in the mid-eighteenth century to describe the district where the merchants and artisan classes lived. To today's Tokyoites, *shitamachi* conjures up images of Asakusa, Ueno, Yanaka, and Nezu. In the days of Old Tokyo the area was a byword for liberalism, freedom, and good times, where the shops, teahouses, theaters, and brothels crowded the main streets, while day laborers lived crammed in labyrinthine alleyways.

In summer, wind-chime sellers peddled their wares from alley to alley. In the winter, noodle stalls operated around the clock, catering at night to people who needed something hot and nourishing after a late night out. Seasonal festivals and events held at neighborhood shrines governed the pattern of *shitamachi* days. On the streets, things were always happening: fighting, impromptu gambling, bursts of laughter from the barbershops and public baths where men hung out, smoking and trading stories.

Up until World War II, *shitamachi* folk carried on the great tradition of "not giving a damn about tomorrow," while their maxim "never carry cash to tide you over the night" was considered the height of fashion. Until the 1940s, the older locals would proudly declare they had never gone further than a hundred yards out of the neighborhood. The world began with the grocers' morning salutations (they often took orders door-to-door) and ended with a jaunt to the neighborhood theater at night, or perhaps a good gossip with friends from next door. During the long summer nights people sat on little bamboo benches that were installed outside every doorway, as smoke from mosquito coils curled into the air.

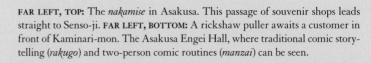

FAR LEFT, TOP: The *nakamise* in Asakusa. This passage of souvenir shops leads straight to Senso-ji. **FAR LEFT, BOTTOM:** A rickshaw puller awaits a customer in front of Kaminari-mon. The Asakusa Engei Hall, where traditional comic story-telling (*rakugo*) and two-person comic routines (*manzai*) can be seen.

THIS PAGE, LEFT: In Asakusa, Tokyo's traditional sweets are displayed with typical downtown flair: a stand for Japanese-style snow cones (*above*), and rice crakers arrayed in glass cases (*middle*). **BELOW:** The foreign visitor's favorite take-away gift: T-shirts decorated with Japanese motifs; here, *kanji* characters for *ichiban* and *samurai*, as well as sumo wrestlers.

Excitement rises to fever pitch at Asakusa's famed festival, the Sanja Matsuri. The Sanja is one of the oldest festivals in Tokyo, and probably the most popular. The spectators flooding the streets literally merge with the *matsuri* participants; combined with the summer heat and the general level of breathless excitement, the experience is similar to being thrown in a sauna, only much more fun. The Sanja is also an opportunity to observe Tokyo downtown machismo firsthand. Most other days of the year, the menfolk are, for the most part, quiet and well behaved; during the festival, they become Wild Things. They don the traditional happi coats (passed down from father to son) and tie the *hachimaki* towels around their heads. Chanting and sweating under the weight of the *mikoshi* (*matsuri* float), they assume a vigorous image of masculinity.

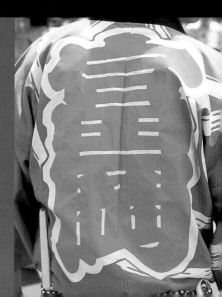

The American bombing of Tokyo in March 1945 literally wiped out the entire *shitamachi* area and destroyed one hundred thousand lives. The bridges crossing creeks and rivers flowing through the network of downtown districts were obliterated, canals were choked with corpses, houses were blown apart, and fires raged everywhere. Novelist Kafu Nagai wrote of hurrying down to Yanaka at that time to inquire after a friend. But when he got there, he said, he was "standing before a huge, flattened and burnt-out wilderness. Nothing was left. It was just blackened earth, as far as my eyes could see."

But just as *shitamachi* bore the brunt of Tokyo's destruction, it was also where the recovery began. True to its inhabitants' indomitable spirit, black-market stalls first went up in Ueno, and to this day the strip of stalls affectionately called Ameyoko attests to the chaotic fervor of that time.

Toughness and pragmatism defined the *shitamachi* spirit, but such virtues were no match for Japan's frenzied march to modernization. The Tokyo Olympics in 1964 and the subsequent period of rapid growth accelerated the destruction of many *shitamachi* values: alleyways and canals came to be seen as unsanitary while the narrow streets were unsuited to trucks and cars. Of course the bamboo benches disappeared. What corporate soldier had time to sit around on a summer night and gossip?

Through the 1960s and '70s, most of the canals were obliterated to make way for the Metropolitan Expressway, while the few that remained became so polluted bubbles of methane rose on the surface. To deal with the problem the Tokyo metropolitan government built "razor walls"—narrow slabs of concrete along the banks of the Sumida River. This was a crippling blow to the *shitamachi* lifestyle, as water had not only been the main source of transportation but also of entertainment and solace. Deprived of the riverways and choked by fumes, *shitamachi* as its people knew it, died. Shop owners moved out to the suburbs and commuted to their workplaces, which became simply that: workplaces.

By the mid-eighties even the workplaces began to disappear. With land prices soaring virtually by the week, real-estate developers moved in to buy up property after property, leaving in their wake a trail of small dirt lots that looked, from above, like cavities in a mouth. *Sento* closed down, cafés were converted into pachinko parlors, and it seemed as though the sound of bulldozers never stopped. The money flowed in, land prices continued climbing, and analysts predicted that by 2001 *shitamachi* would be swallowed up in a dazzling, sci-fi cityscape. One of the landmark projects of the times is the Asahi Beer building in Asakusa, designed by Phillippe Starck and resembling some snarky, modern art installation: a huge black structure topped with a golden cloud intended to recall beer froth.

Potted greenery at Asakusa's lantern plant and wind-chime market, a downtown tradition that dates back four centuries and takes place every July.

ABOVE: Good-luck ornaments on sale at an end-of-year Tori-no-ichi Market. Tokyo's merchants believe that one of these ornaments will see them through during the end-of-year rush, and usher in a prosperous new year. **LEFT:** Geishas choosing a *hagoita* (Japanese racket toy) for New Year's. In the old days, it was the custom for all young women to buy a *hagoita* in December so they could play with them during the new year. Today, a more ornamental version might be found in the home.

ABOVE: The façade of Asakusa's famed Komagata Dojo restaurant. RIGHT: Sampling the *dojo* eel pot at Komagata Dojo. Considered one of the finest delicacies of Tokyo *shitamachi* cuisine, the *dojo*, a small eellike fish, used to be an important source of protein for the Japanese, who only began to incorporate meat and dairy products in their diets in the early twentieth century.

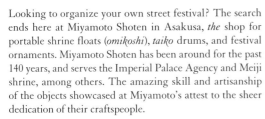

Looking to organize your own street festival? The search ends here at Miyamoto Shoten in Asakusa, *the* shop for portable shrine floats (*omikoshi*), *taiko* drums, and festival ornaments. Miyamoto Shoten has been around for the past 140 years, and serves the Imperial Palace Agency and Meiji shrine, among others. The amazing skill and artisanship of the objects showcased at Miyamoto's attest to the sheer dedication of their craftspeople.

OVERLEAF: Strolling under the cherry blossoms in Ueno Park. Wherever there are cherry blossoms, there are people.

It didn't quite happen that way. When the bubble burst in 1991, it had two dramatic effects on *shitamachi*: First, the developers froze in their tracks, and next it spurred spending on public works. The result was that neighborhoods that had been mapped out for destruction remained intact, and the razor walls that separated Tokyoites from the Sumida finally came down, replaced by parks and low fences. In the mid-nineties, the Tokyo metropolitan government moved to clean up the river, and polluted sludge was shoveled up from the waters and carted away.

As more fish returned, so did the fishermen, and on weekends people were again able to cast their lines and picnic on the banks—a practice once considered impossible to revive. And as the river began to live again, picturesque Japanese river boats became popular for parties and gatherings, and ferries began operating around Asakusa.

Still, the passing years show that Tokyo's *shitamachi*, while still a reality, is also a marketing concept. It is possible to discern a tiny network of alleys, a corner tofu shop that dates back generations, the smoke rising out of a *sento* chimney, camellias sprouting out of a plastic bucket next to—yes—a wooden bench. But it takes looking behind the glitter of the main streets.

If anything has remained fully intact, it is the mind-set. *Shitamachi* people have always said that times are tough one way or another, and the important thing is to live for the moment: tonight's ball game, tomorrow's festival, the passage of the seasons. Grudges, long-lasting emotions, too much passion—these are considered tacky and unrefined. To hang on to something, whether it's a house, a neighborhood, or a way of life, is just not chic. Things will happen the way they happen, and there is little to be done except let the river carry everything away, gather up your resources, and start over.

LEFT: *Shitamachi* is also home to some of Tokyo's best artisans. Meet Mr. Miura, whose hands craft the most amazing objects. **THIS PAGE:** *Jizo* statues (*right*) and a typical downtown shopfront (*below*).

The best sights of Tokyo's *shitamachi* are almost always found in the back streets.
LEFT: These lovely patterned papers (*chiyogami*) are on sale at Isetatsu, a Tokyo
fixture. **ABOVE:** *Shitamachi* residences, with modern vehicles tucked against
traditional wooden façades. **RIGHT:** Inside Nezu shrine.

Boating on the Sumida River, then and now.

SUMIDA RIVER, RYOGOKU

Caught in the hectic cycle of Tokyo life, it is easy to forget that this is a city built on and around water. The broad Sumida River, which divides the city between east and west before merging with Tokyo Bay, has been a source of sustenance, solace, and transport for inhabitants since the city first began to seriously expand in the early seventeenth century. During the Edo period (1603–1868), the city's culture bloomed and developed around the Sumida. The river and its many bridges were the favorite motifs of *ukiyo-e* artists, Kabuki plays almost always featured the Sumida, and various seasonal festivals were held on its banks. Until the 1960s, the river was the city's main support system; when mass industrialization polluted the river beyond recognition, it seemed that a good part of Tokyo as people knew it died too. The fumes rising from the water grew so bad the metropolitan government declared war and corralled the river with a tall, gray concrete wall.

LEFT: It is said that the clashing of wrestler to wrestler should be witnessed in the flesh; only then will one fully appreciate the beauty and power of sumo. **BELOW:** You know you are in Ryogoku when even the bridge decor is about sumo wrestling. **BOTTOM:** An old *ukiyo-e* (woodblock print) from the Edo period depicting sumo. Back then, large men were considered minor deities and conveyors of prosperity. **RIGHT:** The opening ceremony for a day's wrestling features the reigning *yokozuna*.

In the 1990s, however, that same government began to throw money into public works, and one of the projects was to clean up the river, take down the wall, and make the waters accessible once more. Now, as in the old days, Tokyoites pass hot summer nights on Sumida banks to watch the fireworks burst against the sky and feel the breeze come flowing over the water. People can hold parties and gatherings on the *yakata-bune* (chartered river boats) that serve dinner and are fully equipped with karaoke systems. Or they can take the ferry from point to point, and watch the city drift lazily by. The Sumida is still not the cleanest of rivers, but fish that had supposedly fled or died off have returned and so have small flocks of fireflies. With a living, functioning river in their midst, Tokyoites are able to enjoy and discover the city in a way that they haven't done in decades.

Ryogoku, which was one of the few areas to be spared the concrete wall, has always prospered on the banks of the Sumida. The area has been sumo territory for over three hundred years, and the Kokugikan sumo stadium is one of the city's proudest buildings. Sumo, like everything else in Tokyo, has periods of boom and bust, but Ryogoku remains steadfastly loyal to the stables, the stable-masters, and wrestlers. A Ryogoku specialty: all-you-can-eat restaurants that delight in seeing people gorge to their heart's content. Many of these places will not charge the customer if they can manage to eat, say, one hundred dumplings in one sitting. In sumo-town, girth is good.

The Tokyo Metropolitan Expressway is suspended above the beautiful Nihonbashi Bridge, once deemed the very heart of Tokyo.

PREVIOUS PAGE: Fireworks on the Sumida River, a summer pastime in Tokyo for close to three centuries.

GINZA, NIHONBASHI, TSUKIJI

Tokyo locals like to say that the best of their city is concentrated in the Ginza/Nihonbashi/Tsukiji district, that the essence of Old Tokyo somehow remains crystallized on these streets and in the air. Indeed, elsewhere in Tokyo the blocks belong to giant corporations and I.T. entrepreneurs, but this part of town is still run by merchants and small, brand-name retailers that have been around for the past century or more. Most prominent among them are the department stores that line the main strip in Ginza. These used to be snobbish, exclusive businesses operated by prestigious merchant families; now they have evolved into some of Japan's most glitteringly futuristic outlets. Ever in step with the times, landmark department stores have joined hands with foreign luxury brands, converting much of their floor space into sectioned boutiques bearing the logos of Louis Vuitton, Hermes, Tiffany's, and other renowned brands.

Turn left at Mitsukoshi Department Store toward the Kabuki Theater and in ten minutes you'll reach Tsukiji, the wholesale fish and produce market otherwise known as the "kitchen of Tokyo." Tsukiji market (which happens to have been moved en masse from Nihonbashi one hundred years ago) supplies over seventy percent of the city's restaurant and food services. The famed tuna auctions that take place here and start at the crack of dawn every morning have now achieved an iconic status on par with crowded commuter trains. The tuna auction is hard and fast and brimming with cash; at peak seasons, the bidding may reach two million yen for a whole tuna. Navigating one's way through the crowded market stalls and listening to the cries of the hawkers, it is easy to see that as far as fish (and food in general) is concerned, Tsukiji sets the city's gastronomic standards. And old-timers will tell you that the quality of the fish speaks volumes about the state of the economy. Legend has it that the wholesalers here had predicted Black Monday two weeks before it hit the stock market: buyers had become less aggressive, and the quality of the catch being brought in had become markedly inferior; the whole feeling was one of fatigue and laxness, which in the fish market often indicates a prelude to disaster.

東海道
五拾三次
之内

日本橋

In Nihonbashi, the ways of the old have quietly survived, right into the twenty-first century. **CLOCKWISE FROM ABOVE:** Merchants crossing the old Nihonbashi Bridge in the Edo period. Some were likely as not carrying Japanese scissors and cords used to bind the sash on kimonos. Traditional *obi*-tying cords for kimono, quality metalwork, hand-carved toothpicks, and classic patterns stenciled on silk, cotton, and hemp cloth.

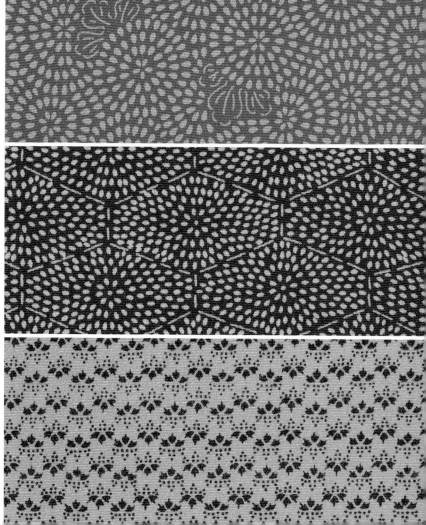

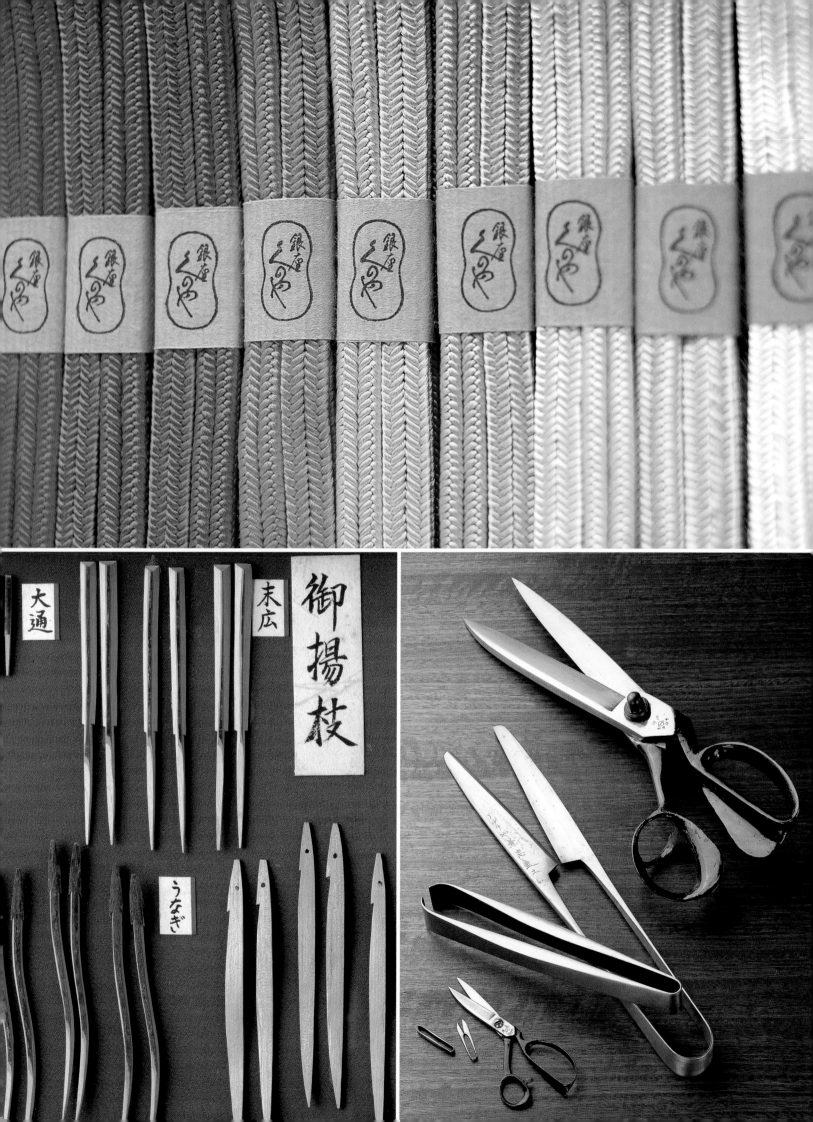

On the way back to Ginza from Tsukiji stop at the Kabuki Theater; the back streets surrounding it form a veritable cocoon of tradition and history. Once you wander into this little oasis, the busy cacophony of the main street (trucks bound for Tsukiji are bumper to bumper) disappears. Time seems to freeze in the tiny, low-ceilinged establishments that have catered to, and supported, the Kabuki arts for over two centuries. Kimono retailers, secretive restaurants, saké shops, and gemlike coffee shops (you'll see the waiters bearing cups on a silver tray and hurrying to the theater's back door entrance) form an urban microcosm enshrouded in drama and mystery.

Stroll back to Ginza, turn right at Mitsukoshi, and go straight along the main street for about a mile (1.6 kilometers) to reach the heart of Nihonbashi: the walk is a guided tour of Tokyo's urban development plan since the end of World War II. This whole area, a bustling but elegant commercial district for three centuries, was almost completely obliterated by the American bombings. Out of the ashes and rubble emerged the infamous Tokyo Metropolitan Expressway, built directly over the town's many canals and the beautiful Nihonbashi Bridge, originally set in an arc and designed to offer a view of Mt. Fuji in the far distance. With the expressway and industrial expansion, the city's waterways became clogged, tall buildings sprung up, and Mt. Fuji disappeared from sight. To deal with increasing pollution, the municipal government choked off the canals and paved many of them over with concrete. Deprived of the waterways and the boats that had been a major source of transportation, Tokyoites were forced to turn to the automobile. The Nihonbashi merchants, who had shipped their goods up and down the Sumida River via the neighborhood canals, switched to trucks. This was a time when Japanese car manufacturers were experimenting with cutting-edge models that would in later years dominate world markets. So just like that, the old was replaced by the new and the rest, as they say, is history.

LEFT: Gateway to paradise. Kanetanaka is one of the nation's most famed restaurants but also a well-kept Tokyo secret. A meal here is an other-worldly experience designed to appeal to every one of the five senses. TOP LEFT: A single lantern and display of flowers welcome the visitor. True to a traditional Japanese restaurant, the doorway is underlit, while inside the lighting is designed to enhance and highlight the fare. TOP RIGHT: A sample of Kanetanaka's artful food arrangements. RIGHT: The shrimp tempura at Ginza's Ten'ichi, renowned for its tempura, seems ready to float off the plate. BELOW: Visitors to Ten'ichi can sit at this splendid lac-quered counter and be served by the chef.

PREVIOUS SPREAD: The main strip in Ginza, where luxury-brand shopping has reached art-form status.

LEFT: Luxury on display: window-shopping in Ginza. **RIGHT AND FAR RIGHT:** In Ginza, groomed and ready for action. Once the bastion of conservatism, Ginza in recent years has become much more attuned to needs of the young and hip. The brands remain the same but the buildings are snazzier and more futuristic, and the number of ultramodern bars are on the rise.
BELOW: One of the surest ways of judging the economy is to count the number of taxis cruising the streets of Ginza. A lot of occupied cabs bodes well for the stock market.

Despite such a backdrop, a hint of the past still lingers mainly because the old businesses (many of them spanning four generations) continue to do business, facing down the bombings, massive urban redevelopment projects, and the high-tech revolution, not to mention economic booms and recessions. And the fact is that the old merchant families in this town have always been among the most progressive and liberal thinkers in Japan. Far from rejecting the new, they consider it, weigh it, and ultimately embrace it. By rejecting the old in favor of the newer, younger, and fresher, modern Tokyoites are said to have emulated the ways of these Nihonbashi merchants. They know that in the ever-changing winds of the Japanese economy, discarding the old is one of the ways of self-protection; if profit and continuity come at the expense of change, then so be it.

Today, the town has become a shopper's paradise and one of the city's most visible tourist hot-spots. Tokyoites say, though, that to stroll around these streets requires a certain state of mind, not just because of the prices (which can get pretty steep) but because it has traditionally been a place where everyone has donned their Sunday best and adopted their best behavior. On weekends the main strip, officially called Chuo Dori but known more commonly as Ginza Dori, is closed off to cars, and the various shops put out parasols, tables, and chairs for pedestrians to have a sit-down. Ice cream vendors toot their horns and street performers compete for attention. Families and couples dressed in varying degrees of chicness and respectability stroll slowly down the avenue. During the Christmas season the Ginza strip is packed with shoppers, and the crowds that throng the counter at Tiffany's (located on the first floor of Mitsukoshi Department Store) is a globally reported consumer phenomenon. Tokyoites talk of the "Ginza therapy"—whatever else is happening in the world, a walk in Ginza will soothe those jangled nerves, and apart from an emptied wallet nothing bad can ever happen here.

LEFT: The Kabuki Theater, inside and out. TOP RIGHT: On stage, a Kabuki extravaganza. Two scenes from the famed play *Sukeroku*. ABOVE: Sukeroku, the most fashonable guy in Edo, decks himself out in full regalia (including the umbrella) to go and visit his lover, who is a high-ranking courtesan in Yoshiwara (the brothel and geisha district). RIGHT: Sukeroku and his lover, one of Kabuki's most famous couples.

LEFT: Tuna on the auction block at the crack of dawn in Tsukiji. **RIGHT AND BELOW:** Sushi as an art form. A plate from the famed Kyubei restaurant in Ginza. Sushi chefs in places like Kyubei apprentice for years before they can actually stand behind the counter. The handling of rice and fish requires the most delicate touch, and a vast knowledge of seasonal fare, the state of fishing, and the different combinations for serving.

At a shrine in Kanda, the names of various fire-fighting units from the Edo period are carved into the stone railings.

KANDA, AKIHABARA

Tokyo has always been in various stages of schizophrenia but nowhere are the symptoms so neatly visible as in the Kanda/Akihabara area. Kanda, the fortress of bookish intellectuals and sanctuary of printed matter, lies elbow to elbow with Akihabara, shrine of I.T. products and consumer electronics.

For close to a century now Kanda has been home to some of Japan's oldest and most prestigious universities, and the small side streets as well as the main strips teem with bookstores. Some are large, five-storied affairs with glass elevators and others are immersed in the precious and rarified atmosphere of the second-hand book dealers. Browsing and book-hunting become positive pleasures, especially when followed by a jaunt to any of Kanda's legendary cafés. Dark, small, and smokey, these places are full of dedicated print addicts sipping strong coffee and fortifying themselves for more hours of pavement stomping with heavy carry bags in tow. Many a poet and novelist has written of the sheer joy and sensory satisfaction that comes of strolling in Kanda, and of the first rip of wrapping paper as the bookworm goes home and tears into his newly acquired purchases. Words, words, words: sometimes the very air in Kanda seems to smell of print ink.

In Akihabara, such antiquated pleasures are obsolete—in fact, they have never existed. The town originally emerged as a black market lot in the immediate postwar years and then evolved into *the* place for discount home appliances. As Tokyo rushed headlong into the modernization/rapid growth era during the 1960s and '70s, Akihabara's huge neon signs attested to the city's indomitable optimism, love of technology, and progress. As manufacturers launched one new, dazzlingly convenient appliance after another, eager consumers from around the nation (and across the ocean) came to bask in the white-hot fervor of Akihabara's florescent lights.

Ever in step with Tokyo's societal values, Akihabara has reinvented itself once again, into a veritable giant microchip. The wares in the shops are almost all I.T. related, and plans are underway to link Akihabara and Tsukuba in Ibaraki Prefecture (home to Japan's space agency) with a superexpress train service. When that happens the nation's most advanced engineers will be commuting back and forth between their labs and high-tech city. The scenario is practically a science-fiction cliché.

In the Edo period, Kanda and Akihabara were roughly considered one and the same district, and guarded by the famed shrine Kanda Myojin. One of the most powerful and prominent of all Edo shrines, it was said that walking here on the average weekday was difficult because of the large number of fellow worshippers, but during the big festivals it was an impossibility: the crowds multiplied to such an extent that pickpockets had a field day, incidents of spontaneous crime soared, and women and children were freqently trampled

At the shrine Kanda Myojin, home of the local gods.

underfoot. Kanda promised fun and excitement and adventure but it was not exactly the place for the weak and frail.

In the very masculine city of Edo, Kanda was renowned for carrying male aesthetics to extremes: the back streets were full of clandestine gambling hovels placed strategically near drinking establishments and brothels, and on the main streets men were often seen in heated arguments or impromptu fist fights.

The phrase "He's from Kanda" implied the person had a dangerously short fuse, but at the same time was loyal, generous, manly, and hard-working. To this day, people born in Kanda seem more Tokyoite than other locals, and there are many in the elder generation who claim you can always tell a Kanda-born from their facial features: decidedly fiery. Whether this still holds true is open to debate but in many of the small printing houses and bookstores, the merchants do seem different—-for one thing they don't have that air of excessive politeness that often defines the Tokyo service industry.

Interestingly, the same applies to Akihabara sales-clerks. They are informative and quick on their feet, but they refuse to kowtow to the customers, probably because they are well aware of the superiority of their products and confident that the customer *will* buy. (Witness the number of people carrying boxes with laptops and rice-cookers.) Besides, come festival time every Kanda and Akihabara merchant knows they can out-shout and out-drink any other Tokyo local right off the streets.

Kanda offers the comfort of history and whiffs of the past from the pages of musty books; Akihabara will always be in pursuit of the next brain-cell jiggling phenomenon. Take your pick, and start walking.

RIGHT: Kanda's most popular cuisine: handmade soba noodles at the restaurant Matsuya.

RIGHT: Nicolai Cathedral, Tokyo's only Russian orthodox church, located near the Kanda River. **BELOW:** The Kanda River at Ochanomizu Station.

A sliver from Akihabara, a page out of Kanda. **LEFT:** The typical Akihabara shops are plasticky, multitiered theme parks dedicated to the art of selling electronics in bulk and as cheaply as possible. **BELOW:** Rare hardcovers and first editions on display in one of the many bookshops in Kanda, the hangout for intellectuals, collectors, and nostalgia fans.

The back streets of Kagurazaka are famed for their cobblestones, exclusive inns, and secluded restaurants.

KAGURAZAKA, KORAKUEN

If Kagurazaka were a woman she'd be an actress—not young but shrewd and experienced and adept at playing any role required of her. And indeed, this has always been a feminine sort of town, home to geisha houses and the geisha-related businesses like drinking establishments, small and exclusive *kappo* (Japanese-style restaurants) frequented by power politicians, and the various small industries that support their operations. At the same time, Kagurazaka has nurtured a liberal, internationalized ambience through its French bookshops, Italian and Asian restaurants, and arthouse movie theaters. Would-be engineers from the nearby Tokyo Science University, tramp up and down the hill, Tokyo's Francophiles gather at the Japan-Franco Institute, and lovers converse while looking out at Kanda River from the popular Canal Café. At heart Kagurazaka is adamantly conservative, sticking to the traditions and values of a century ago. However drastically the surrounding areas may change, she remains protective of the cobblestoned alleyways, the tiny cafés, and the confectionary shops whose twin distinctions are history and longevity. Remember, though, that she is an old and practiced hand in the ways of the world; if you think Kagurazaka is nothing but quaintness and charm you may be in for a surprise.

A ten-minute walk brings you to Korakuen, where the Tokyo Dome City complex conjures up a scene straight out of a Phillip K. Dick novel. This used to be an unruly, teeming sort of area crammed with *yakitori* stalls, second-hand book shops dealing in pulp and porn, small businesses, and cheap restaurants. Now it basks in the glitter of the forty-three-storied Tokyo Dome Hotel and joyous cacophony from the adjacent amusement park and Tokyo Dome stadium. The hotel is ever-popular among newlyweds who stay here

for their honeymoon and couples who want to play in the amusement park by day and relax in the nearby, newly built spa by night. During baseball season, families from all over Japan come to cheer at the stadium, Japan's first indoor sports arena. In recent years, the Dome has also become a hotspot for events and concerts; many a visiting celebrity musician has insisted on performing here. Tokyoites say an evening in Dome City can provide one with enough entertainment mileage to last the next six months, but the Tokyo governor, who has made Korakuen one of his most visible projects, has professed dissatisfaction. Korakuen needs more facilities, more people, more businesses! So what's in the works? The blueprints for a giant casino complex to rival the main strip in Las Vegas are being evaluated.

LEFT: Inside the exclusive Kagurazaka restaurant Yuki-moto. **ABOVE:** The temple Zenkoku-ji enshrines Bishamon-ten (Vaisravana), one of the four guardians that protect the realm of the Buddhas. Bishamon-ten has been popular since the Edo period. **RIGHT:** *Zori* for women and *geta* for men, both footwear for kimono, on sale at Sukeroku, which opened for business in 1910. The elegant *zori* are for formal occasions, and *geta* for casual ones.

PREVIOUS PAGE: In May, the Japanese iris offers a feast for the eyes at Korakuen Garden.

Tokyo Dome, Japan's first indoor stadium, is also home to the Tokyo Giants, the team closest to the heart of most Japanese males. Just as American ballplayers aspire to the Yankees, Japanese players pine to join the Giants. In recent years, the team has also become a launchpad to playing in the American major leagues.

Strolling under gingko trees on
Gaien Dori near Omotesando.

OMOTESANDO,
SHIBUYA, SHINJUKU

"When I come here, I become a raging insomniac. It's a case of stimulus overload." So said a French clothing designer of his response to Shibuya, the vortex of Tokyo's youth/pop culture. This is where it all begins, and then ends: the various fashions, trends, and booms that come and go faster than you can say "Karl Lagerfeld."

Walk down the famed Centaa-gai (Center Street), a narrow side strip hemmed in on both sides by outrageous teen-fashion boutiques, cacophonous fast-food joints drenched in florescent lights, and video game centers blinking neon and streaming digitalized rap music nonstop. Be prepared for the visual onslaught of Tokyo's teens—in a society renowned for politeness and restraint, the under-nineteen crowd here seem to have arrived from another planet. This cellphone-toting, hot-dog devouring crowd in bizarre makeup and customized school uniforms comprise the most important segment of Tokyo's consumer market. Retail analysts comb their hang-outs weekly to tune into their vibes and zero in on the next Big Thing. Every new shop that opens here does so after careful consideration of their tastes and demands. This is a town where the adult caters to the child and capitalism takes on a whole other aspect: to make it in Shibuya requires juvenile tastes and the aura of irresponsibility. It's not surprising that the most successful entrepreneurs in Shibuya look like teenagers: small, slender, utterly casual, and totally irreverent.

One of them is Nigo, the designer of a quintessentially Shibuya brand: A Bathing Ape. Though Nigo himself was born outside Tokyo, as soon as he hit his early teens he began taking weekly two-hour train trips into Shibuya to get a feel of the streets and shop in the district's legendary boutiques. At the age of nineteen he became a fashion writer and by his early twenties he was working as a magazine stylist. Now in his early thirties he is one of the most visible and successful of Shibuya business icons, so wealthy that he freely admits to not knowing what to spend his money on anymore. It can't be *Star Wars* paraphernalia: he has the whole collection.

One subway stop away is Omotesando. The crowd here is a little older and more sophisticated; they saunter up and down the tree-lined avenue carting many shopping bags bearing the logos of the world's most expensive luxury brands. These brands have, for all intents and purposes, taken over the main strip: Gucci, Louis Vuitton, Prada, Chanel—whatever else is happening to the Japanese economy seems to have little effect on the shopping habits of Omotesando.

And blending a little of each is Shinjuku, home to the Park Hyatt Hotel made famous by Sophia Coppola's movie *Lost in Translation*. The New York Grill, where Scarlett Johansson and Bill Murray exchanged quips over drinks, continuously appears among the Top Ten best bars/eating establishments in Tokyo and offers a resplendent, 360-degree view of the city. The Park Hyatt by the way is also the best place to see Mt. Fuji from the inner city—looming in the distance like a sci-fi hologram.

If Shibuya is Kiddyland and Omotesando is the domain of monied madams plastered with designer logos, Shinjuku is, in part, the stomping grounds of the over-thirties crowd and the Japanese "salaryman" on the prowl for drinks and pleasure. Shinjuku is a theme park of back street pubs, basement jazz clubs, and *yakitori* joints. It also has Kabuki-cho, with front-row seats to the goings-on inside Tokyo's sex industry, with everything from costumed S&M to more refined, Oscar Wilde–like games shaded by literary fancy.

LEFT: The precincts of the shrine Meiji Jingu, built by volunteers to honor the Meiji emperor; at Harajuku Station, in Shibuya Ward. ABOVE AND RIGHT: Tradition and ritual are nurtured with care in the confines of Meiji Jingu.

Lesser known but even more intriguing is nearby Shin-Okubo, a.k.a. Tokyo's Little Asia. Teeming with Thai, Vietnamese, and Korean restaurants, with signs in five different Asian languages (some are Russian), this is one area where Japanese is decidedly *not* the main spoken language. Shin-Okubo is now one of the most feverishly exciting spots in Tokyo, and a genuine immigrant town that's free from both tourism logistics and many of the restrictions of the city's economy. The wonderful news is that in Shin-Okubo one can get stuffed to the eyeballs with genuine Southeast Asian cuisine and drinks, and then sober up in a streetside café—for under three thousand yen.

The Shinjuku experience is quite a formidable slice of the Tokyo pie—it really should have a warning sign about indigestion.

LEFT: Luxury brands are as familiar as the zelkova trees—Omotesando's twin icons. **THIS PAGE, ABOVE:** Teenybopper Central and marketing phenomenon—a typical Shibuya street scene with crowds and neon. **RIGHT:** Shinjuku's new face—buildings and more buildings.

Tokyo grandeur reaches new heights
with the advent of Roppongi Hills.

ROPPONGI, AOYAMA

Elsewhere in Tokyo foreign visitors may find themselves some-
what at a loss, perhaps even alienated. But in the Aoyama/
Roppongi area, they will feel right at home. Indeed, on week-
end nights it seems there are more foreigners than Japanese. Even
the people distributing fliers on the intersections are often hefty,
cheerful Americans, who as likely as not will wish you a "great time"
after offering directions to, say, the Hard Rock Café.

Roppongi is a postwar invention, an area that became hip and
expensive mainly because the shops and watering holes did business with the G.H.Q. It wasn't long before the youth scene shifted
from downtown Tokyo to this west end, and the postwar generation who danced, sported ponytails, and drank Coca-Cola, con-
vened at the jazz bars, and ate spaghetti at the famed Chianti, one
of Japan's oldest Italian restaurants at the tip of Roppongi. During
the 1980s the town spawned Tokyo's disco and club culture, and
people wearing anything less than a sizzling designer outfit were
bounced at the doors with ceremonial disdain.

The eighties were also the salad days for Japanese fashion. Each
season designers and stylists would fly en masse to Europe to test-
run their work on Paris and Milan runways. Their boutiques were
located in Aoyama and had hushed, sacrosanct atmospheres. People who shopped here were more like worshippers, offering prayers
(and alms) at the altar of Japanese fashion. The rule was that you
bought your clothes in Aoyama boutiques by day (quiet and well
behaved) and showed them off in Roppongi clubs by night (raucous
and decadent). It was a convenient arrangement.

Now Aoyama's brand of chic is less snobbish and more genuine, but somehow that doesn't mean those invisible walls have come crumbling down. Roppongi can be duplicated: its blend of foreign embassies, luxurious expat condos, bars, and underground sex shops all unfolding against the backdrop of Tokyo Tower—it is not an unfamiliar setting in urban Asia. But Aoyama strikes a different pose, and there is something Zenlike about the severe buildings with their clean, straight lines, as well as the slender, monkish populace who walk by dressed all in black. Aoyama ends too, with the Nezu Institute of Fine Arts, famed for its pristine Japanese garden and staunch refusal to display anything but East Asian art. The Institute sets special store on the tea ceremony (the founder was a tea ceremony connoisseur) and there are several tea houses located in the garden, open to use by various masters and their disciples. On weekends, kimono-clad ladies can be seen in the garden, seated on the waiting area adjacent to the tea houses, while inside the master prepares a precise and exquisite setting.

That two neighborhoods so completely different as Aoyama and Roppongi exist in harmony, offers one of the best examples of Tokyo's unique ability to defy logic.

FAR LEFT: Love it or hate it, the twenty-seven-foot spider by the ninety-three-year-old sculptor Louise Bourgeois is instantly memorable. FAR RIGHT: A glass chair by Tokujin Yoshioka adds an artistic accent to the street scene in Roppongi. TOP: Aoyama blends fashion with a quiet mystique. LEFT: Not to be outdone, Tokyo Tower turns on the lights. It is still one of Tokyo's most beloved landmarks.

The Nezu Institute of Arts is not exactly high-profile but has enough ardent fans to ensure its place as a secret Aoyama trademark. The visitor is captivated by the fine collection of East Asian art and the hushed, zenlike atmosphere.

The Nijubashi Bridge outside the Imperial Palace.

IMPERIAL PALACE, MARUNOUCHI

The Imperial Palace has always headed the list of Tokyo's Seven Wonders. There exists, right in the heart of this teeming megalopolis crammed with towering architectural monstrosities, an immense, 277 acres (112 hectares) of lush forestry surrounded by a four-hundred-year-old moat. Somewhere beyond the trees, deep inside the forest, is the palace itself. No one has ever been allowed into the grounds except under the most extreme and honored circumstances. Visitors can stroll on the gravel of the outermost limits and look at the gates, but the rest of the Imperial Palace (meaning all of it) remains an impenetrable mystery. And so rumors abound as to what lies beyond the green water and stately trees: Tokyoites have long speculated that the grounds are a botanical paradise where near-extinct species of plants, insects, and animals have found sanctuary. Some say the cherry trees are the finest in Japan, yielding blossoms so dense and multihued they no longer resemble cherry blossoms but some elegant tropical flower. After all, the Imperial family are renowned horticulturists and nature-lovers; the late Emperor Showa is said to have ordered that not a single tree branch be tampered with, and consequently the palace forest has spawned its own, unique ecosystem.

Unlike western castles and monuments that impress the viewer with their might and splendor, the Imperial Palace is about the nothingness of space. Foreign visitors are sometimes confounded by the absence of anything to *see*, and many a frustrated tourist with a camera has been heard to exclaim: "But there's nothing here to photograph!" The Japanese, on the other hand, stand on the pathways and let their imagination venture beyond the gates and into the forest. The elder generation will be seen bowing, with their eyes closed; their reverence is toward something hidden, obscure, and probably very precious.

The area that surrounds the Imperial Palace in a half-loop is Marunouchi, Tokyo's most prestigious business and financial district. This territory had once been the exclusive domain of Japan Inc.'s top-notch companies; now, thanks to urban development projects, Marunouchi has been reinvented as a hybrid of commerce and fashion. The world's most prominent designers have installed boutiques on these streets as well as Tokyo's hippest restaurants and cafés.

The change was a gradual one, starting in the mid-1990s and reaching a temporary peak with the opening of the New Marunouchi Building (a huge, thirty-six stories of some of the city's most impressive and exciting restaurants, boutiques, and offices) in 2002. Tokyoites gasped at the audacity of a New York–like skyscraper so close to the Imperial Palace (in another age, this would have been unthinkable, for no Japanese was allowed to view the palace from above) and at the same time embraced the concept of a new Marunouchi with cautious delight.

The town's businessmen were, at first, less happy with the changes. After all, Marunouchi had been a bastion of Japanese conservatism, where casual conversation meant topics like golf or yesterday's ballgame (baseball, not soccer), and anyone seen wearing jeans on the dark gray pavement was considered either in the throes of temporary insanity, or a visitor from another planet. Businessmen

LEFT: Boating under the cherry blossoms in the old castle moat. ABOVE: The streets of Marunouchi at dusk. RIGHT: The New Marunouchi Building is crammed with fashion, fine dining, and events.

were appalled at the idea of suddenly having to share their turf with youths who strolled by clutching take-out frappucinos from Starbucks and sporting not just one, but many pierced earrings per ear.

Soon, however, they caught on to the fact that maybe the redevelopment and the subsequent reshuffling of street demographics was not such a bad thing. Besides, the frappucinos were good, and many companies were introducing weekly "casual days," encouraging older employees to relax and dress down a little. Maybe even try on a pair of jeans.

The result: a wary but peaceful coexistence. Elsewhere in Tokyo the populace is categorized and divided according to profession and social status; here, the stern, suited corporate soldiers walk side by side, and get in coffee lines with the likes of models, artists, and designer jet-set types. An intriguing blend.

The famed red-brick façade of Tokyo Station's Marunouchi Exit. Erected in 1914 by Japanese architect Kingo Tatsuno, this was one of Tokyo's very first modern public architectural projects, and remains to this day one of the city's most recognizable landmarks. There is even an adjacent hotel (the Tokyo Station Hotel) that has become a metaphor for romantic, Tokyo-style classicism, and that has miraculously managed to survive the wave of redevelopment.

PART II

HISTORY

Tokyo is often described as the anti-Kyoto—everything for which the ancient capital stands (tradition, sensitivity, subtlety) speaks of all that Tokyo is *not*. In 1867, when the emperor was forced to relocate from Kyoto to what was then described as "that Eastern epicenter of barbarism," his aides and ministers wept for fear that the strong dusty winds, which swept through Old Tokyo (then called Edo) at the beginning of each season, as well as the less-than-refined Eastern cuisine, and the severe and manly landscape would all prove too grievous for the imperial family.

Indeed, Tokyo has always been described as a rude and masculine city, as opposed to the gentler Kyoto. But then Tokyo was a distinctly masculine invention. For centuries prior to 1603 (when the city was officially established), the nation had been fragmented by constant warfare. It was then that the cunning and tenacious Tokugawa Ieyasu (1543–1616) outsmarted his rivals and seized power once and for all in the Battle of Sekigahara in 1600. He then appointed himself shogun (commanding general) of Japan and installed the government within the confines of the Edo Palace. Ieyasu came to Edo earlier, in 1590, when was designated lord of the entire Kanto Plain by the national hegemon Toyotomi Hideyoshi (1537–98). The new appointee decided to make Edo his headquarter. At that time, Edo was a coastal village supporting less than one hundred small wooden houses with thatched roofs. Ieyasu, was shrewd enough to see the area's potential, believing it had a great future because the land was fertile and its climate was mild. Further, he thought the rivers crisscrossing the region would be ideal for transporting goods and other items for a growing city. He soon started several river improvement projects and the city became prosperous; as a result, its population swelled to over 150,000 by 1609.

Ieyasu set about cementing his authority by making Edo and the rest of Japan impenetrable. He cut off all relations with the outside world and either expelled or executed all foreigners (including merchants and missionaries). Travel was restricted to those with passes, and women were basically forbidden to move from their neighborhoods. All the regional lords were forced to live in Edo residences, or leave members of their immediate family in Edo; they were allowed to return once a year to their home territories in an expensive, time-consuming journey with an entourage befitting their rank, an enterprise designed to drain funds which could otherwise be used to raise an army. All this was to ensure stability and prevent any possibility of a coup.

Portrait of the shogun Tokugawa Ieyasu.

Procession of a *daimyo* lord, who rides in the covered palanquin guarded by his men.

Nihonbashi, at the center of the Japanese capital city of Edo, awash with foot traffic above and boat traffic below. By the eighteenth century, Edo boasted a population of one million. (From the *Illustrated Guidebook of Edo* [*Edo Meisho zue*] published in seven volumes from 1834 to 1836.)

At the same time, the shogun fostered a samurai culture based on stoicism, loyalty, and nonconfrontational masculinity. The samurai class was taught that to do battle and cause a stir was shameful; any urges to be violent were to be directed toward oneself. This became the ritual of *seppuku*, or suicide by disembowelment, the mainstay of the Tokugawa rule. Because of this custom, Edo and the rest of Japan existed in peace for the next 250 years and Edo became prosperous, and the most densely populated city in the world.

The Tokugawa status quo was shattered when Commodore Perry and his black ships paid a visit to Edo, and in 1854 forced the nation to open its gates. Little more than a decade later, the shogun relinquished the reins of power to the emperor, Edo was renamed Tokyo (meaning Kyoto of the East), and the samurai class collapsed in the face of a new social order. A mad rush for modernization/Westernization began and the nation threw many of the old customs and traditions out of its first glass windows. Tokyo became the stage for all that was new, experimental, and exciting within twenty years: the nation had its first café, ballroom dance floor, Western-style restaurant, bakery and creamery, as well as Western-style house with genuine bathroom fixtures. By the early 1900s the Japanese were wearing top hats and suits, and had become contenders in international politics. Tokyo was known as one of the most expensive cities in the world.

Today, the equation has not changed much. Tokyo, still one of the most expensive places to be, remains a work-in-progress. Ever intent on reinventing itself, the scrap-and-build method of urban development has become a way of life. A clutch of buildings is torn down and replaced with a towering skyscraper, whole neighborhoods are razed to make way for glittering new office complexes and condominiums. It is hard to pinpoint any identifying landmarks when the Next New Thing seems to emerge every three months. Maybe this Kyoto of the East is still the obnoxious bad boy, but at least it is never dull.

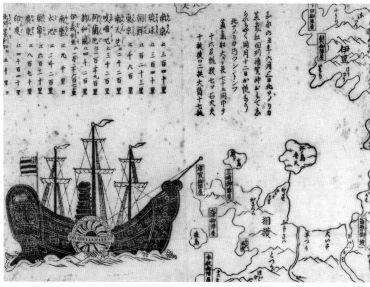

This map shows the black ships of Commodore Perry arriving in Uraga (Kanagawa Prefecture), rousing Edo out of nearly three hundred years of insulated peace and prosperity.

TRANSPORTATION

Tokyo is huge and sprawling. There is no easy way to cover the length and breadth of its varied sights, though every means of public transportation known to modern man is available—from the monorail that extends to Haneda Airport (the hub for domestic flights), to the intricate bus lines that crisscross the city like blood vessels, to the ships that bear divers away to Tokyo's resort islands. The furthest are the Ogasawara Islands, six hundred miles (one thousand kilometers) away and offering the kind of lush, untouched scenery one might associate with Maui. To the west, you can take the Japan Railways (JR) train for a hike on Mt. Takao. Way out to the east, the subway goes to Chiba Prefecture. Nowhere on earth is the term "getting away from the city" more difficult to realize.

Tokyo's transportation network, growing increasingly convenient (and ever more detailed) over the years, is linked to the capital's many development projects. For City Hall, an architectural marvel designed by the renowned Kenzo Tange, a new subway station was built. It is never enough to build office buildings and

Consumer electronic shops cram the central street of Akihabara.

shops in Tokyo; people must be able to reach them by public transportation or the facilities will sink into obscurity. In some cases, destinations that can only be accessed by car or on foot have been able to enjoy an exclusiveness all their own, and have come to be referred to by Tokyoites as city hideaways. But it is difficult to find such places anymore. Take the Azabu Juban neighborhood, one of Tokyo's oldest and best-kept secrets. An inner-city enclave that boasts a genuine natural hotspring and tiny, family-owned shops, Azabu Juban now teems with high-rise condos and tourists thronging the main strip, solely because of its new subway station. Old-timers say that the enclosed, snug feel is gone and the community has subtly changed. Indeed, with its high-rises and slick coffee and burger chains, Juban has become a Tokyo town much like anywhere else.

Even so, Tokyoites are extremely proud of the intricate and infallible (barring extreme weather conditions) transportation system. The first thing a newcomer does upon reaching the city is to get hold of the train network map and trace the best way to reach the workplace or go to Akihabara (the electronics and home appliances town). With a tourist map in hand, they will also note the stations that seem surrounded by the most interesting-looking streets and shops. And even after years go by and that person becomes a Tokyo local, finding new ways to navigate the city at lower cost or in less time becomes his or her secret hobby. The same goes for the average born-and-bred Tokyoite who makes it a point to stash a small subway map in their wallet. In Tokyo, everyday is a journey.

LIFESTYLE

One of the enduring Tokyo myths goes something like this: the people here work too hard and are always in a rush, but they are never rude. Even as far back as 1610, Japanese travelogues to Old Tokyo (then called Edo) describe how "these people in the East" were far too industrious and diligent for their own good but, that said, they were surprisingly "generous, humorous, and clear of mind."

Tokyoites are also known for their ability to forget grudges and move beyond the negative, in other words, to get on with their business with little complaint. This is the Tokyoite's greatest strength and most palpable weakness. In their haste to forgive and forget, Tokyoites have let the city be overrun by non-Tokyo entrepreneurs and politicians who have teamed up with giant contractors. Together, these "outsiders" have plunged the city into a vicious construction cycle of scrap and build, which means that everyday, somewhere in the city, yet another neighborhood is being razed to make room for a huge glass, chrome, and concrete monstrosity. The bulldozer has become one of the city's most visible icons, and the gritty crunch of buildings and houses being torn down is one of the most familiar sounds.

At the same time, Tokyo is a surprisingly green city and one of the greatest pleasures is to stroll under lanes of old zelkova, gingko, or cherry trees and be astonished at the trilling of birds or the singing of crickets in such an urban setting. The love of greenery is a Japanese trait but it is also very Tokyo and speaks volumes about the lifestyle here. Because living conditions have never been easy, Tokyoites have learned to take comfort in small pleasures, and to seek beauty in the mundane. As a result, seasonal flowers and shrubbery adorn most doorsteps and windows and the most beautiful of trees can grow out of the most miniscule patches of earth in an obscure backyard.

The other Tokyo specialty is ditching the border between work and play, between stress and relaxation. Businessmen are known to put in incredibly long office hours (a twelve-hour day is considered slack in many major companies) but those hours are tempered by coffee-shop breaks, ninety-minute lunches, a quick beer at six, between meetings. When work breaks at nine or ten, people head out for karaoke and a bowl of noodles before boarding the train for home, where most can count on a home-cooked, midnight dinner. Tokyo businessmen are often pitied by the rest of Japan and the world, but these same businessmen will tell you that they actually enjoy a sense of freedom not found elsewhere; the freedom to live close to the street, to cultivate favorite watering holes unknown to the family, and to make the day stretch out for as long as possible. And let's not forget that many (though fewer than before) Tokyo businessman enjoy a job security that, in spite of the recession, still holds strong. All this fuels that traditional Tokyo optimism: whatever happens today, tomorrow will always be a brand new day.

FOOD AND DINING

The Tokyoite's appetite for food borders on gluttony—and a lot of the time the dividing wall is perilously close to being demolished. Food from every remote corner of the globe is available here, from Kenyan frog soup to Mongolian horse-milk pudding: you name it, Tokyo's got it and the people will eat it faster than you can say "revolving sushi." Of course, it hasn't always been like this. In fact, it has only been about five decades since the average Tokyoite could afford to consume three square meals a day: the city endured a three-year famine during World War II followed by the lean, postwar years when women traveled to the countryside to trade their most treasured kimonos for rice with which to feed their families.

That does not alter the fact that the city has always loved to eat, and eat well. After Japan opened its doors to the West in the mid-nineteenth century, Tokyo took center-stage in producing (and sampling) exotic foreign cuisines previously unheard of in the Japanese gastronomic glossary. The capital built the nation's first cafés, was the first to experiment with hamburgers, and tinkered with the Indian curry so that it would suit the Japanese palate. Such undertakings spawned the advent of the Tokyo gourmand, renowned for being fussy, discerning, and always on the quest for new taste sensations. It is little wonder, then, that Parisian establishments like La Tour D'Argent, Maxim's, and Taillevent opened their first Asian outlets in Tokyo, which also has the reputation for the best Italian food this side of the Pacific.

The obsession with food also means the Tokyoite's appetite goes through cycles—French nouvelle cuisine swept the city in the 1980s, followed by authentic Italian in the nineties, and Thai, Vietnamese, and designer Indian food (*not* just curry) in new millennium. Meanwhile, Tokyo has always loved to fuse Japanese sensibilities with whatever cuisine is in vogue, and the city now has an increasing number of fusion restaurants helmed by adventurous chefs experimenting with dishes like fresh salmon-and-scallion spring rolls, caviar sushi, squid-and-cod-roe pasta.

The Tokyoite is also fashion-conscious to a fault, and after some scary reports on the alarming increase of the Japanese girth, people have learned to balance their meals. This means fish rather than meat, lots of veggies, less grease. The advent of Japanese-style vegetarian restaurants indicates how the Tokyo fling with food has come full circle: after having gorged on pretty much everything, the most enticing fare now seems to be that once-scoffed-at traditional Japanese menu of brown rice, miso soup, and a vegetable dish. Young women go in for "beautifying food" and are extremely sensitive to anything that is fattening or damaging to the skin. This is why, instead of going out for pizza, they will choose to have lunch at the popular Onigiri Café franchises, where one can get a flawlessly aesthetic tray of rice balls, soup, pickles, and decaffeinated tea (total calories: 380) for under 500 yen. In the end, Tokyo dining boils down to options, options, options!

TOKYO'S POP-CULTURE

What draws people to Tokyo? It can't be the weather (on a good year, we get over one hundred days of rain), or our relaxed and laid-back lifestyle (are you kidding?), or the prospect of riches (stay tuned for more about the recession). And unless you are Bill Murray and Scarlett Johansson in *Lost in Translation* (and even they had a hard time of it), this is not exactly the city of love. So it must be something else. And increasingly, that seems to be stuff like *manga*, movies, art, and music.

Indeed, Tokyo's brand of pop-culture is fast on its way to becoming Japan's biggest export item. Tokyoites have discovered that the rest of the world shares their huge love for *manga* and that most addicting of modern sensory vices; the video game. And even snobs who have turned their backs on cartoons cannot fail to be enthralled by the animated films of Hayao Miyazaki, whose works have consistently received recognition at major international film festivals, inspiring animators around the globe. Every year, an increasing number of people make the pilgrimage to Mitaka, in west Tokyo, where Miyazaki's production office, Studio Ghibli, has built the acclaimed Ghibli Museum, showcasing still photos; stacks of Miyazaki's original, hand-drawn animation stills; merchandising products; and memorabilia. Ghibli's works are known for their strong, sociopolitical messages, and Miyazaki often chooses girls or women (the weaker, less privileged sex) for the main roles. But far from finding glamorous love or becoming princesses, these females learn the value of labor, the importance of independence, and the conviction that work is the only way for them to mature and be truly happy.

But the most fascinating slivers of Tokyo culture are not the kind packaged and exported overseas, but those found among the debris and energy overspill on the streets. One of the best places to witness this firsthand is in Shibuya, where the chaotic energy of high-school kids clashes (and/or merges) with Japan's giant retailers. Together, the kids and the corporations have spawned a unique street culture based on design, consumption, and sex appeal—rather than the more familiar rebellion, violence, and poverty. The kids here may emulate the style and music of New York underground rappers but, at the end of the day, they board the train to the suburbs where, likely as not, their mothers are keeping their dinners warm. The same goes for the teenage girls who peddle their school uniforms and lingerie (and in many cases a lot more) on Shibuya streets: they may congregate in donut shops to do their homework. The kids are not beyond mocking themselves; the girls, all too aware of the short shelf-life of their youthful sexual appeal, once took to making themselves up like old women, putting gray and white streaks in their hair, and wearing mud-colored lipstick. The boys painted logos of Chanel and Vuitton on their standard-issue book bags, mocking their own infatuation with luxury brands. Those same kids will tell you that if a trend can survive here, it can survive anywhere.

FASHION

In the eyes of the rest of the world the Japanese come off as disciplined, quiet, and repressed. That's okay, the Japanese themselves feel the same way; they are constantly berating themselves for their emotional passivity, lack of fiery passion, and the general blandness hovering around them. However, there is one form of dramatic self-expression at which many Japanese excel: the clothes they wear.

Fashion, or more specifically street fashion, is and has always been one of Tokyo's most exciting phenomena. As far back as the seventeenth century the people of this city made subtle social statements through the patterns of their kimonos, the way they tied their sash, their choice of hair accessory. In fact, fashion carried such importance that the government once banned all bright colors and bold patterns for fear such things would breed rebellion. But then the people went right ahead and used those colors and patterns on lining and other areas not readily visible. Chic was redefined: the façade of dark, understated materials over extravagant (and illegal) dyed silk and embroidery became the metaphor for street hip. To this day, the equation applies.

And never let it be said that Tokyo is fashion conservative. Once the city opened its gates to Western influences, the city never stopped experimenting. In the late nineteenth century, combining things like scarves, stand-up-collar shirts, and boots with traditional kimonos was all the rage. In the 1920s women went around with fur capes, earrings, and bobbed hair, and arranged their kimonos to look like the dresses drawn by Alfonse Mucha.

After World War II, Japanese clothing designers emerged, and modernized Tokyo fashion began to flower in earnest. Hanae Mori became the city's "first successful career girl"; she designed clothes for the urban working woman and changed the course of Japanese fashion forever. Such unheard-of contraptions as knee-length skirts, chunky pumps, and masculine suit jackets appeared on the streets and, at the same time, were immortalized on-screen by filmmaker Yasujiro Ozu. On Mori's heels came designers like Issey Miyake, Yohji Yamamoto, and Rei Kawakubo (of Comme des Garçons), all of whom took their work to Parisian and European runways, astonishing crowds with their cerebral and excessively stoic garb that enveloped almost every inch of the female body in various shades of black. Kawakubo went so far as to declare that concealing the body was far sexier than revealing it, and that excessive skin exposure was unseemly, ungainly, and *so* passé.

On Tokyo streets, people were doing fantastic things with their clothing. Teenage girls would deck themselves out in long satin robes embroidered with slogans such as BORN TO FIGHT and I DON'T NEED YOUR OPINION, and offset these with makeup that involved several coats of black lipstick and electric blue eyeshadow.

Unlike elsewhere in the world, Tokyo's fashionistas could strut their stuff on the streets with no worries of being bullied, robbed, or maimed. Visual outrageousness was never a sin or an object of hatred—the worst that could happen to a fashion slave (apart from abject servitude to the chosen name-brand) was to have an empty wallet. Subsequently, impromptu runways emerged all over the city with main avenues on Omotesando and in Shibuya and Shinjuku, the prime domains for fashion watching. Media photographers completed the picture; they could be seen standing every few yards on choice strips, hands poised on cameras and eyes scanning the crowd for the next, hot, undiscovered model.

An induction into Westernized womanhood consisted of imported dresses, shoes, and hats, as well an appreciation for Western music. (From *Singing in a Plum Garden* [*Baien shoka-zu*] by Yoshu Chikanobu, 1887.)

Speaking of which, inner-city Tokyo boasts more professional models (from all over the world) per square foot than anywhere else in the world, a fact which attests not just to the city's ardor for fashion, but the sheer size and density of the fashion industry. Just the number of fashion-related magazines in the Tokyo area adds up to more than the entire total in the European Union; this means more stylists, photographers, editors, designers and—yes—a corps of leggy models stomping the streets bearing portfolios. This is something that just does not happen anywhere else in Japan, not to mention the world. It is no wonder, then, that the recurring, quintessential Tokyo question is not about life, politics, or God but simply: "What am I gonna wear today?"

NOTES TO THE PLATES

PAGES 10–11: **Towering testimony to Tokyo's love for design: the metropolitan government office buildings.** These office buildings are the work of Kenzo Tange, one of the nation's most innovative architects, whose unique views on design and lifestyle changed the urban Japanese sense of space. The view from the top floors offers one of the most exciting vistas in the city and is proof of Tange's strong conviction that Tokyo is best experienced from above.

PAGES 12–13: **Tokyo from above: a maze of lights and high-tech.** During the days of Edo (Old Tokyo), nights were defined by a dense and all-encompassing darkness. Now it is difficult to find a space where it is not all bright light and blinking neon that lasts until the early hours of the morning.

PAGES 14–15: **The famed Kaminari-mon (Lightning Gate) at the entrance to the temple Senso-ji in Asakusa.** The Kaminari-mon gate is protected by two gods, whose fiery wrath is a warning against evil spirits and evildoers. It is very much in the Japanese tradition to combine the spiritual with the purely commercial—once past these gates, a paved walkway hemmed in on both sides by souvenir shops stretches all the way to the temple.

PAGE 16: **The *nakamise* in Asakusa. This passage of souvenir shops leads straight to Senso-ji.** Shops have lined the avenues approaching temples for centuries, many run by the same families for generations.

PAGE 16: **A rickshaw puller awaits a customer in front of Kaminari-mon.** Rickshaws had long vanished from the streets, but in recent years they have returned to select tourist areas. Asakusa's rickshaw pullers comprise some of the best tour guides, equipped with an encyclopedic knowledge of monuments, shops, and Tokyo's historical lore.

PAGE 16: **The Asakusa Engei Hall, where traditional comic storytelling (*rakugo*) and two-person comic routines (*manzai*) can be seen.** Also known as "the art of talking," *rakugo* and *manzai* require years of training and apprenticeship under strict masters.

PAGE 17: **A stand for Japanese-style snow cones.** This summertime treat is a Japanese favorite, and the *shitamachi* area is where you can still get these handmade. The slivers of ice are shaved from huge blocks delivered by Tokyo's few remaining traditional ice companies. A sweet topping is poured over a mound of shaved ice collected in a shallow bowl, then the refreshing treat is eaten with a spoon.

PAGE 17: **Rice crackers arrayed in glass cases.** Asakusa rice crackers are still made the way they always have been—by hand. Artisans sit by a long pit of piping hot charcoal, dip the crackers in soy sauce, and roast them one by one.

PAGE 17: **The foreign visitor's favorite take-away gift: T-shirts decorated with Japanese motifs; here,** *kanji* **characters for** *ichiban* **(number one) and** *samurai*, **as well as sumo wrestlers.** The sumo wrestlers were inspired by old woodblock prints.

PAGE 18: **Excitement rises to fever pitch at Asakusa's famed festival, the Sanja Matsuri.** During the Sanja, you will hear the chant "*seiya, seiya*" or "*wasshoi, wasshoi*." Both are meant to convey *wa*, or harmony, and the goodwill that comes from everyone united in a single task. The men form a circle to carry the *mikoshi*, and when they want to change direction, rotate themselves in a loop so that the circle isn't broken. This is to assure that peace and harmony surround the float.

PAGE 19: Float bearers sport various logos on the backs of their *happi* coats. The patterns and letters may change according to neighborhoods or families (some of the logos are passed down from generation to generation). Just the very act of donning a *happi* coat is said to enhance the strength and concentration necessary to sustain the extreme physical effort of *mikoshi*-carrying.

PAGE 20: **Potted greenery at Asakusa's lantern-plant and wind-chime market, a downtown tradition that dates back four centuries and takes place every July.** The market is a summertime festivity that alleviates the "*tsuyu* (rainy season) blues." People dress in light, summer *yukata*s (cotton kimonos), stroll the market, and prepare for the heat of summer by purchasing wind chimes and plants. Come August, these suggest coolness to the mind and eye.

PAGE 21: **Good-luck ornaments on sale at an end-of-year Tori-no-ichi Market.** Tokyo's merchants believe that one of these ornaments will see them through the end-of-year rush, and usher in a prosperous new year. The Tori-no-ichi ornaments are excessively decorative. In the austere and bare Tokyo home of old, such things were hallmarks of privilege and distinction. The bigger, the more colorful (and adorned with all kinds of charms), the better.

PAGE 21: **Geishas choosing a** *hagoita* **(Japanese racket toy) for New Year's. In the old days, it was the custom for all young women to buy a** *hagoita* **in December so they could play with them during the new year. Today, a more ornamental version might be found in the home.** The *hagoita* of old were decorated with portraits of popular Kabuki actors and geishas. The decoration on the more economical models comprised stenciled portraits, while that on the high-end models (like these) resemble flattened dolls and are in themselves works of art.

PAGE 22: **The façade of Asakusa's famed Komagata Dojo restaurant in Asakusa.** The architecture has remained unchanged for the past 150 years. Visitors go to take photographs of the white *noren* just as much as to sample the fare. Though the small, eellike *dojo* fish is not as popular as it used to be (many young people admit to never having tasted it), Tokyo elders like to say that the taste of burgers is exceeded by that of the more delectable *dojo*: the ultimate fast-food of yesteryear.

PAGE 23: **Miyamoto Shoten has been around for the past 140 years, and serves the Imperial Palace Agency and Meiji shrine, among others.** This portable-shrine float can cost up to 150 million yen and can weigh close to a ton (1,000 kilograms). The Miyamoto logo is proudly displayed just beneath the wings of the falcon, a symbol of masculine strength and endurance.

PAGES 24–25: **Strolling under the cherry blossoms in Ueno Park.** Cherry blossom viewing is more like picnicking amidst swarms of people. It is the tradition to bring lots of food, a blanket to spread on the ground, and—most importantly—big bottles of saké. Getting a bit tipsy under the blossoms with a warm April breeze blowing is a Tokyoite's birthright, as well as being the first real induction into spring, after a cold and windy winter.

PAGE 26: *Shitamachi* **is also home to some of Tokyo's best artisans.** Despite the wave of nanotechnology encroaching on the city, many back streets retain the ways of old. *Shitamachi* artisans like Mr. Miura continue to hone their craft with as much dedication as their grandfathers before them, and the tools they use have changed little over the last four hundred years.

PAGE 27: **Jizo statues.** Artisans are also known for being religious and superstitious—above all, they pray to the gods for stability in the home and strength of body. Accordingly, the *shitamachi* area is full of small, secluded temples and tiny shrines where people can stop off, say a little prayer, and go on their way.

PAGE 27: **A typical downtown shopfront.** A wheelbarrow is parked outside this Buddhist flower shop. Stores such as this are usually found just outside cemeteries, so visitors may buy a seasonal bouquet to adorn the gravestones of their loved ones and ancestors.

PAGE 28: **These lovely patterned papers (***chiyogami***) are on sale at Isetatsu, a Tokyo fixture.** The designs date back four hundred years or more. The patterns are, from left to right, a clever hybrid motif of crabs and peonies, a playful display of spring radishes, and a stylized rendition of chain links.

PAGE 28: **A** *shitamachi* **residence, with modern vehicles tucked against the traditional wooden façade.** The typical *shitamachi* scenery comprises an old wooden house with a modern vehicle parked right outside. Some *shitamachi* residents prefer retro models for their cars, perhaps to complement the street scene.

PAGE 28: Outside a typical *shitamachi* house. Tokyoites are renowned for their green thumbs and are avid gardeners, even when deprived of an actual garden space. Often, a few pots and a chunk of earth is all that they need.

PAGE 29: **Inside Nezu shrine.** Nezu shrine is one of the oldest in Tokyo and boasts a collection of azalea bushes that bloom in glorious splendor every May. Each pair of poles makes up a *torii* (entrance gate for the gods) and are erected with donations from local shop owners and worshippers.

PAGE 30: This *ukiyo-e* (woodblock print) by Utagawa Toyokuni III shows a boating party of women at Ryogoku. The monied and privileged often chartered boats to watch the fireworks during the summer, and the cherry blossoms in the spring.

PAGES 30–31: **Boating on the Sumida River.** Since the metropolitan government moved to clean up the Sumida, boats and boat-lovers have returned to the waters. Though it is no longer used as a source of everyday transportation, there are few experiences that match the pleasure of zipping up and down the Sumida on a small, rapid ferry. These are flat, hunched contraptions, because the bridges on the Sumida are generally built low.

PAGE 32: **It is said that the clashing of wrestlers should be witnessed in the flesh; only then can one fully appreciate the beauty and power of sumo.** Sumo practice is all about training the body to endure the mighty weight and pain of other bodies crashing into one's own. The sound of muscles slapping against one another is the definitive sumo sound.

PAGE 32: **You know you are in Ryogoku when even the bridge decor is about sumo wrestling.** The decor shows a *yokozuna*, or reigning champion wrestler in a ceremonial pose.

PAGE 32: **An old *ukiyo-e* (woodblock print) from the Edo period depicting sumo. Back then, large men were considered minor deities and conveyors of prosperity.** In the Edo period, the average Japanese were much smaller than today, and consequently people had much greater reverence for large men. It was said that if you fed and then gave saké to a sumo wrestler, wonderful luck would stay with you for the rest of your life.

PAGE 33: **The opening ceremony for a day's wrestling features the reigning *yokozuna*.** To become a *yokozuna* requires skill, dedication, and practice, practice, practice. Interestingly, body mass will help though it is not the deciding factor—some of the greatest *yokozuna* have been (relatively) small men.

PAGES 34–35: **Fireworks on the Sumida River, a summer pastime in Tokyo for close to three centuries.** Japan boasts some of the world's best and most skilled firework artisans, and one of the perks of living in the city is being able to view their creations firsthand. Summer is not complete without the boom and crackle of fireworks in the distance, followed by the sight of a majestic flower blazing in the sky.

PAGES 36–37: **The Tokyo Metropolitan Expressway is suspended above the beautiful Nihonbashi Bridge, once deemed the very heart of Tokyo.** In the Edo period and until the 1960s, it was possible to view Mt. Fuji from this bridge. The building of the expressway right over it was a subject of heated debate, but *shitamachi* aesthetics wound up bowing to the tide of change and corporate logic.

PAGE 38: **Merchants crossing the Nihonbashi Bridge in the Edo period.** *Ukiyo-e* print. The men in the center are carrying wooden basins of fish, as the city's fish market used to be located in Nihonbashi, before moving to Tsukiji.

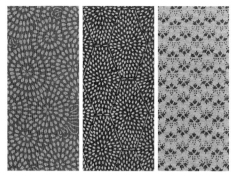

PAGE 38: Traditional patterns, called *Edo-komon,* are used for kimono fabrics, bags, towels and other household products. Hand-dyed in classic colors, the motifs depict the chrysanthemum (left and center) and the paulonia (right).

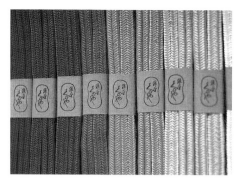

PAGE 39: *Obi*-tying cords for summer kimonos on display at Kunoya, which has been doing business in Ginza since 1837. Sash holders, though less visible than the actual sashes, are one of the things Tokyo women love competing over. The colors and textures vary from shop to shop but all the holders are handmade.

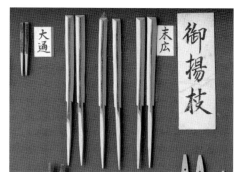

PAGE 39: Toothpicks are handmade with incredible attention to function and detail at Saruya in Nihonbashi, which first opened shop in 1704. As was the custom three hundred years ago, the toothpicks still have various names and are categorized according to their various uses. For example, one would not use the same kind of toothpick to pierce a piece of fruit or a pastry as for oral hygiene purposes.

PAGE 39: There is nothing quite like Japanese scissors for touch and sheer beauty of form. These are on sale at Nihonbashi's Ubukeya (opened in 1783), where the master scissors-maker assures his clients that scissors, properly looked after, will last several generations.

PAGES 40–41: **The main strip in Ginza, where luxury-brand shopping has reached art-form status.** In recent years, the brand shops in Ginza have shifted from high-end domestic to European. Many of the select European luxury brands have opened up shop in Ginza, transforming it from a quintessential Tokyo commercial district to international boutique central.

PAGE 42: **Gateway to paradise. Kanetanaka is one of the nation's most famed restaurants, but also a well-kept Tokyo secret. A meal here is an otherworldly experience designed to appeal to every one of the five senses.** Kanetanaka values taste and presentation above all else. Foreign visitors are often surprised by the small portions, but impressed by the speed and timing of the appearance of each dish, so artfully presented and precisely heated. Like French cuisine, the point is to enjoy and partake of a sensual experience rather than merely satisfy one's hunger.

PAGE 43: **Visitors to Ten'ichi can sit at this splendid lacquered counter, and be served by the chef.** Ten'ichi is a quality tempura restaurant that opened in 1930, and after his first visit there Frank Sinatra made it de rigueur to drop in each time he came to Tokyo.

PAGE 44: **Luxury on display: window-shopping in Ginza.** Though Ginza has toned down its snobbishness, it is still Tokyo's designated, luxury-shopping area. This window display shows a snug, streamlined jacket: a favorite among Tokyo femmes.

PAGE 45: Even in Ginza, franchise coffee shops, discount sushi restaurants, and fast-food outlets are on the rise, but Ginza fans will tell you service here still means having a polite young person pour your tea from an immaculate porcelain pot.

PAGE 45: The famed Chanel building on Ginza's Namiki Avenue. This thoroughfare, a few streets away from the main strip and lined with trees, has a stately, European ambience.

PAGE 45: The new Apple flagship store that opened in Ginza in 2003. Four stories of Mac computers, gadgets, and a genuine Genius Bar staffed by multi-lingual Mac whizzes to solve all your Mac-related problems.

PAGE 45: The new Salvatore Ferragamo building, reputed to showcase the latest and best of Tokyo architectural skills. Outside, it is hip and high-tech, but the shoes on display are all about old-world elegance.

PAGE 45: **One of the surest ways of judging the economy is to count the number of taxis cruising the streets of Ginza. A large number of occupied cabs bodes well for the stock market.** When times are bad, businessmen will pack it in early and catch the last train. When cash flow is good, they stay around for one more round and go home by cab.

PAGE 45: Ginza bars used to mean brightly lit lounges presided over by hostesses, but recently more people like to frequent the hip, cozy places that are well designed and affordable.

PAGE 46: The exterior of the Kabuki Theater, first erected on this spot in 1889. The original building was renovated in 1923, and then burned down in the firebombings of World War II. It was reconstructed in 1951.

PAGE 47: Kabuki comes from the word *kabuku*, which means a cutting-edge attitude. This is why Kabuki plays are peopled by characters who, like Sukeroku, aspire to the very edge of dandified chic, with an attitude to match today's rock stars. In the scene with his lover, Sukeroku tells her that he is about to avenge the death of his father. She advises him to wait for the right opportunity, since acts of violence in the Yoshiwara district were heavily punished, sometimes by execution. Sukeroku is played by Danjuro Ichikawa XII, his lover by Jakuemon Nakamura.

PAGE 48: **Tuna on the auction block at the crack of dawn in Tsukiji.** Tuna auctioning accounts for the tensest moments at the Tsukiji market, for tuna prices are a deciding factor in the day's sales volume, and can be a general indicator of the state of the economy.

PAGE 49: **Sushi as an art form, as practiced at the famed Kyubei restaurant in Ginza.** High-end sushi is defined by the precise pressure of the chef's fingers, applied to the rice just so. This particular style of sushi is called *Edo-mae*, or Old Tokyo style. In times past, a true Tokyo sushi chef refused to use fish that was caught outside Tokyo Bay. Now that no longer applies, but they still insist on the best and freshest of fare.

PAGES 50–51: **At a shrine in Kanda, the names of various fire-fighting units from the Edo period are carved into the stone railings.** Firefighters were heroes of Old Tokyo and symbols of masculinity, bravery, and strength. Various units were stationed all over the city but Kanda, renowned for its many fires, had numerous such units.

PAGE 52: A rooster proudly stands on a festival *taiko* drum. This wagon forms part of the procession in a festival whose central feature is the *mikoshi* float carried by locals to invite the gods of prosperity to descend on the town.

PAGE 52: **At the shrine Kanda Myojin, home of the local gods.** A couple pose for a wedding photograph in front of the shrine. Though church weddings are popular among young people, some Tokyo couples like to get married the old-fashioned way, in the local shrine.

PAGE 53: **Kanda's most popular cuisine: hand-made soba noodles at the restaurant Matsuya.** This antiquated building has been declared a cultural treasure, and inside people can be seen sipping saké and downing soba noodles any time of the day or night.

PAGE 54: **Nicolai Cathedral, Tokyo's only Russian orthodox church, near the Kanda River.** The Nicolai Cathedral is home to the Japan Halistos Orthodox Church, founded in 1862. In 1994, plan were drawn up for the church to be renovated, which took nine years to complete. The building, as seen in the photo, is now one of the most beautiful stone architectural structures in Tokyo.

PAGE 54: **The Kanda River at Ochanomizu Station.** Boats go up and down the river, which here runs parallel to the JR (Japan Railways) tracks, offering commuters a visual respite.

PAGE 55: **The typical Akihabara shops are plasticky, multitiered theme parks dedicated to the art of selling electronics in bulk and as cheaply as possible.** Functionality and speed overshadow aesthetics in Akihabara. This has spawned a particular kitsch culture all its own. Shopfronts aim to amuse and astonish, while signs that often display nothing more than product names are plastered all over the windows.

PAGE 55: **Rare hardcover and first editions on display in one of the many bookshops in Kanda, the hangout for intellectuals, collectors, and nostalgia fans.** In Kanda, one browses for rare editions in the sanctimonious atmosphere of the second-hand book dealer. These shops are often presided over by cantankerous old merchants, renowned for their short tempers, gruff manners, and encyclopedic knowledge of printed matter.

PAGES 56–57: **The back streets of Kagurazaka are famed for their cobblestones, exclusive inns, and secluded restaurants.** The Wakana Inn, on the left, has always been a favored haunt of Japanese novelists. Armed with just sheets of paper and a fountain pen, the literati would hole up in one or the other of Wakana's rooms and churn out the next bestseller over the course of a few weeks. Yuki-moto (featured on PAGE 58) is one of only nine exclusive restaurants remaining in the area.

PAGE 58: **Inside the exclusive Kagurazaka restaurant Yukimoto.** Yukimoto opened for business in 1948, when Tokyo was recovering from the devastation of World War II, and is now run by the third generation of the same family. Until 1990, drinking parties with geishas were common. Today, less than half of the customers call for geishas, and Yukimoto puts more emphasis on food. In the traditional full course, approximately ten dishes are served.

PAGE 59: **The temple Zenkoku-ji enshrines Bishamon-ten (Vaisravana), one of the four guardians that protect the realm of the Buddhas. Bishamon-ten has been popular since the Edo period**. The gates are protected not by the familiar statues of dogs, but by a pair of lions.

PAGE 59: *Zori* for women and *geta* for men, both footwear for kimono, on sale at Sukeroku, which opened for business in 1910. The elegant zori are for formal occasions, and geta for casual ones. An Internet site has brought more customers to this traditional shop, with its wide selection of footwear. Although it is unlikely that women will return en masse to the kimono lifestyle, the kimono and its paraphernalia have become fashionable once more.

PAGES 60–61: **In May, the Japanese iris offers a feast for the eyes at Korakuen Garden.** You would never know you were in Tokyo, once inside the city's numerous botanical gardens. The Korakuen Garden dates back 350 years and was once a vacation spot for samurai lords. The iris was a favored flower among the samurai, who used the leaves in tea and bathwater to build strength and nurture courage, while the flowers often adorned their tea ceremonies. The iris and the cherry blossom are both representative of Tokyo flora and metaphors for masculinity and stoicism.

PAGES 62–63: **Tokyo Dome, Japan's first indoor stadium, is also home to the Tokyo Giants.** Going to the Dome has an air of celebration about it, and general good cheer hangs over the crowds well before the game starts. The Tokyo Giants have been playing baseball here since 1937. Next to it is the Ferris wheel in Korakuen Amusement Park.

PAGES 64–65: **Strolling under gingko trees on Gaien near Omotesando.** While Omotesando has its zelkovas, the neighboring Gaien Dori avenue has the gingkos. After the cherry blossoms, one looks forward to the gingko trees in May. Gingko branches adorn themselves in thick, pungent leaves of the darkest green that gradually turn golden in the autumn sun.

PAGE 66: **The precincts of the shrine Meiji Jingu, built by volunteers to honor the Meiji emperor; at Harajuku Station, in Shibuya Ward.** The main *torii*, or entrance to the house of gods (the biggest in Japan), is shown here in all its majesty. Because the shrine was erected to honor the Meiji emperor, the imperial crest of the chrysanthemum is prominently featured.

PAGE 67: **Tradition and ritual are nurtured with care in the confines of Meiji Jingu.** Here, the various assistants to the priests line up to pay their respects to the shrine.

PAGE 67: A horseman shows his skill in Japanese archery, once the favored sport of both the imperial family and Tokugawa shogunate. The tournament is open to visitors and offers a window on bygone times.

PAGE 68: **Luxury brands are as familiar as the zelkova trees—Omotesando's twin icons.** On the main strip in Omotesando, luxury shopping means shopping for European brand names. Old apartment buildings were torn down and in their place emerged French and Italian boutiques.

PAGE 68: Male elegance reaches a new peak of snobbishness in this shop window featuring British-styled gentlemen's suits.

PAGE 69: **Teenybopper Central and marketing phenomenon—a typical Shibuya street scene with crowds and neon.** The Q-Front Tower just outside the train station is one of Shibuya's most visible landmarks. Every week, the ranKing and ranQueen billboard lists the top-selling products among teenage boys and girls.

PAGE 69: **Shinjuku's new face—buildings and more buildings.** Shinjuku, in all its commercial splendor. On the left is the Takashimaya Department Store (the largest floor space in Japan) and in the center is the NTT Docomo building.

PAGES 70–71: **Tokyo grandeur reaches a new high with the advent of Roppongi Hills.** Roppongi Hills is part of Tokyo's most ambitious redevelopment project. A complex of offices, condominiums, restaurants, and boutiques, the Hills, as people refer to complex, is a mini-city designed to fulfill every requirement of daily city life. It is one of the most design-conscious spaces in Tokyo.

PAGE 72: **Love it or hate it, the twenty-seven-foot (eight-meter) spider by the ninety-three-year-old sculptor Louise Bourgeois is instantly memorable.** The Frenchman's sculpture—made from bronze, stainless steel, and marble—has turned out to be one of the most talked-about features of the Roppongi Hills complex, which is full of postmodern sculptures like this one.

PAGE 72: **A glass chair by Tokujin Yoshioka adds an artistic accent to the street scene in Roppongi.** According to designer-artist Yoshioka, the chair all but vanishes in the rain. The thick glass panels were cast using the same sophisticated techniques called on for fashioning high-quality lenses for today's mega-telescopes.

PAGE 73: **Aoyama blends fashion with a quiet mystique.** High-end luxury brand shops are laid out with understated elegance in small, back-street squares. Such urban enclaves are an Aoyama specialty.

PAGE 73: **Not to be outdone, Tokyo Tower turns on the lights. It is still one of the city's most recognizable landmarks.** Tokyo Tower was built in 1958, in the astonishing span of just eleven months. A few feet taller than the Eiffel Tower in Paris, it became the symbol of the rise of Japanese technology and economic growth.

PAGES 74–75: **The Nezu Institute of Arts is not exactly high-profile but has enough ardent fans to ensure its place as a secret Aoyama trademark. The visitor is captivated by the fine collection of East Asian art and the hushed, Zenlike atmosphere.** A prominent piece in the collection is this pair of six-panel screens, which show irises from a scene in the *Tale of Ise*. The artist is Ogata Korin (1658–1716), one of the foremost painters in the Edo period and a master of intricate brushstrokes and bold color schemes. *Tale of Ise*, a well-known love story of Heian period (794–1185), has inspired many painters and provided them with themes for their works. Korin painted the bridge scene from the story without people, bridges, and streams. Instead, he relied on a rhythmical placement of irises that allows the viewer to imagine the bridges.

PAGE 74: The pathway leading up to the front entrance of the Nezu Institute of Arts. The walk along the path is in itself an experience. The institute is also renowned for its Japanese garden, laid out below the museum. Since the founder was a tea ceremony connoisseur, the garden has a number of teahouses.

PAGE 75: Inside the teahouse Ichiju-an, a tea master has laid out the service for the tea ceremony. It involves nothing more than a teacup, a kettle for hot water, a ladle, a small container of tea leaves, and a single morsel of Japanese confectionary.

PAGE 76: **The Nijubashi Bridge outside the Imperial Palace.** The Nijubashi Bridge is a symbol of imperial dignity as well a testament to Japanese architectural skills just after the country opened up to the West. The gentle arc below the bridge, and its reflection in the water, has been lauded as one of Tokyo's most beautiful images.

PAGE 78: **Boating under the cherry blossoms in the old castle moat.** The view from Chidoriga-fuchi, a famed beauty spot for cherry blossoms and boating outside the Imperial Palace. In the distance is the roof of the Budokan, where the likes of Dylan, Nirvana, and Madonna have held concerts.

PAGE 79: **The streets of Marunouchi at dusk.** Commuters throng the pavement of Marunouchi in the evening, likely as not heading back to the office. To work here is a badge of distinction, and the privilege to enjoy the fruits of one of Tokyo's most tasteful urban development projects.

PAGE 79: **The New Marunouchi Building is crammed with fashion, fine dining, and events.** The building remains one of Tokyo's most popular urban complexes. Completed in 2002, it boasts thirty-six stories of offices, fashion boutiques, cafés, and some of the city's best restaurants.

PAGE 80: **The famed red-brick façade of Tokyo Station's Marunouchi Exit. Erected in 1914 by Japanese architect Kingo Tatsuno, this was one of Tokyo's very first modern public architectural projects, and remains to this day one of the city's most recognizable landmarks.** Though the area surrounding it has changed beyond recognition, the station building remains the same, which is nothing short of an urban miracle in ever-changing Tokyo.

ACKNOWLEDGMENTS

The publisher would like to express its gratitude to all of the following organizations, companies, and establishments for graciously granting permission to use the photographic images in present volume:

Awaya: page 7, top
Isetatsu: page 28, left
Japan Actors' Association: page 47
Kabukiza: page 46–47
Kanetanaka: pages 42, 43 (top left and right)
Komagata Dojo: page 22
Kunoya, Ginza: page 39, top
Kyubei (sushi shop): page 49
Miura Hiroshi: page 26

Miyamoto Unosuke Shoten: page 23
Roppongi Hills: pages 1, 4–5, 70–71, 72
Sony Corporation & Amazon Incorporated: pages 7, 43, 46 (bottom), 49
S. Watanabe Color Print Co.: page 7, bottom
Saruya, Nihonbashi: page 39, bottom left
Sukeroku: page 59, bottom
Ten'ichi (tempura restaurant): page 43, center and bottom
Tokujin Yoshioka Design: page 72, bottom
Tokyo Dome: pages 62–63
Ubukeya, Nihonbashi: page 39, bottom right
Yukimoto: page 58

PHOTO CREDITS

Hibi Sadao: page 38, bottom three
JTB Photo: page 22, top
Kaji Hiroya: pages 6, 7, 21 (top), 28 (top), 42–44, 46 (bottom), 49
Kato Shoji (Bon Color): pages 60–61
Kodansha Photo Library: pages 30 (left), 38 (top)
Kuwata Mizuho: jacket photo; pages 2–3, 4–5, 10, 11 (bottom), 12–13, 26, 28 (bottom), 30–31, 40–41, 45 (except top right), 46 (top), 54, 64–67, 69–71, 73 (bottom), 76–77, 79–80
Matsunaga Koki: page 11 (top), 48
Nakayama Tsutomu (A. collection, Amana): page 62
Nezu Institute of Fine Arts: pages 74–75
Nihon Sumo Kyokai: pages 32 (top left and bottom), 33
Nonaka Ikuo (Bon Color Photo Agency): photo for book band

Ogawa Tomoko: page 47
Ozawa Hiroyuki: pages 14–15, 18–20, 21 (bottom), 23–25, 52 (top), 53, 56–57, 58, 59
Pacific Press Service: page 11, center
Tanaka Aya: page 73, top left and right
Tankosha: page 22, bottom
Tomioka Mamoru (Sekai Bunka Photo): pages 34–35
Tsuji Tomonari (Bon Color Photo Agency): page 78
Yamada Yuzo (Q Photo International): pages 8–9
Yasuda Sachiyo: pages 1, 16–17, 27, 29, 32 (top right), 36–37, 45 (top right), 50–51, 52 (bottom), 55, 62–63, 68, 72
Yokota Shoichi (courtesy of Tankosha): page 39

Map by Omori Tadamitsu

英文ビジュアル版　東京──江戸の息吹
Seeing Tokyo

2005年6月　第1刷発行
2008年8月　第4刷発行

著　者　庄司かおり

発行者　富田　充

発行所　講談社インターナショナル株式会社
　　　　〒112-8652 東京都文京区音羽 1-17-14
　　　　電話　03-3944-6493（編集部）
　　　　　　　03-3944-6492（営業部・業務部）
　　　　ホームページ　www.kodansha-intl.com

印刷・製本所　大日本印刷株式会社

落丁本・乱丁本は購入書店名を明記のうえ、講談社インターナショナル業務部宛にお送りください。送料小社負担にてお取替えいたします。なお、この本についてのお問い合わせは、編集部宛にお願いいたします。本書の無断複写（コピー）は著作権法の例外を除き、禁じられています。

定価はカバーに表示してあります。

Printed in Japan
ISBN 978-4-7700-2339-1

CHRONOLOGY

JOMON PERIOD   c. 10,000–c. 300 B.C.

YAYOI PERIOD   c. 300 B.C.–c. A.D. 300

KOFUN PERIOD   c. 300–710

552   Introduction of Buddhism from China.

607   First official embassy to China.

645–50   Taika Reform.

NARA PERIOD   710–94

710   Nara becomes Japan's first capital.

752   Dedication of the Great Buddha of Todaiji temple, Nara.

781–808   Reign of Emperor Kanmu.

HEIAN PERIOD   794–1185

794   The capital is moved to Heiankyo (Kyoto).

838   Twelfth and last embassy to Tang China.

995–1027   Supremacy of Fujiwara Michinaga, official of the imperial court.

c. 1002   Sei Shonagon writes *The Pillow Book*, a diary of Heian court life.

c. 1008   Murasaki Shikibu writes the *Tale of Genji*.

1180–85   Genpei War between the Minamoto and the Taira clans, won by the Minamoto.

KAMAKURA PERIOD   1185–1333

1191   The monk Eisen returns from China and founds the Zen sect.

1192   The title of shogun is granted to Minamoto no Yoritomo.

1219   Minamoto no Sanetomo, the third shogun, is assassinated, ending the line of Minamoto shoguns.

MUROMACHI PERIOD   1333–1573

1374–1408   Noh drama flourishes through Kan'ami (1333–84) and Zeami (1363–1443) under the patronage of shogun Ashikaga no Yoshimitsu (1358–1408).

1392   Reunion of the Northern and Southern Courts.

1397   Kinkakuji (Golden Pavilion) temple built by Yoshimitsu.

1542   Portuguese land at Tanegashima, an island south of Kyushu, and European firearms are introduced.

1549   St. Francis Xavier (1506–52) arrives in Kyushu.

1568   Oda Nobunaga (1534–82) occupies Kyoto.

AZUCHI–MOMOYAMA PERIOD   1568–1600

1573   Nobunaga consolidates his power and the fighting ends.

1682   Nobunaga is assassinated by Akechi Mitsuhide; Toyotomi Hideyoshi (1536–98) succeeds him.

1586   Osaka Castle is built by Hideyoshi.

1587   Sen no Rikyu (1522–91) officiates the grand tea ceremony held in Kitano, Kyoto, under the sponsorship of Hideyoshi.

1589   Christianity is proscribed.

1600   Tokugawa Ieyasu (1542–1616) wins the Battle of Sekigahara.